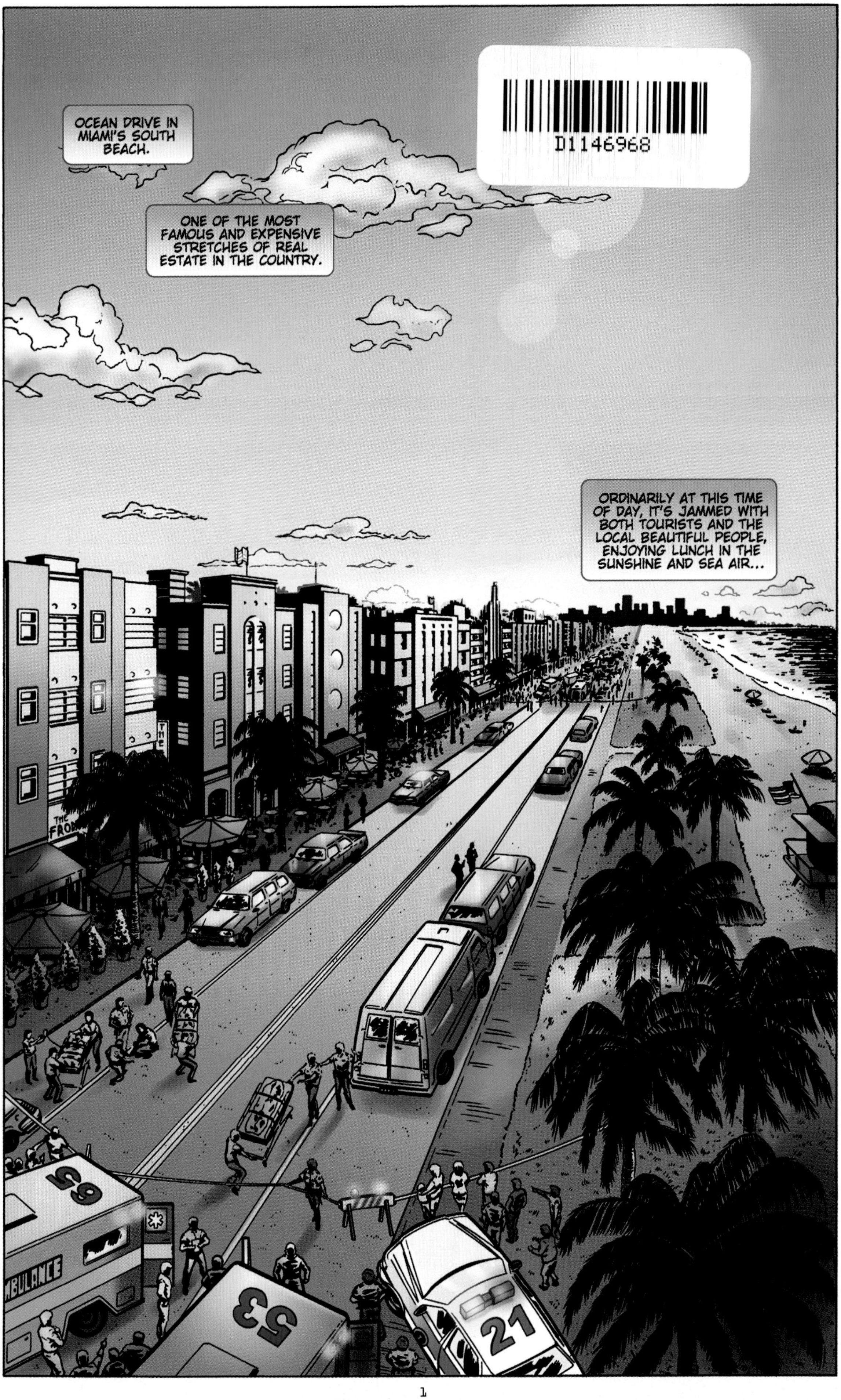
OCEAN DRIVE IN MIAMI'S SOUTH BEACH.
ONE OF THE MOST FAMOUS AND EXPENSIVE STRETCHES OF REAL ESTATE IN THE COUNTRY.
ORDINARILY AT THIS TIME OF DAY, IT'S JAMMED WITH BOTH TOURISTS AND THE LOCAL BEAUTIFUL PEOPLE, ENJOYING LUNCH IN THE SUNSHINE AND SEA AIR...

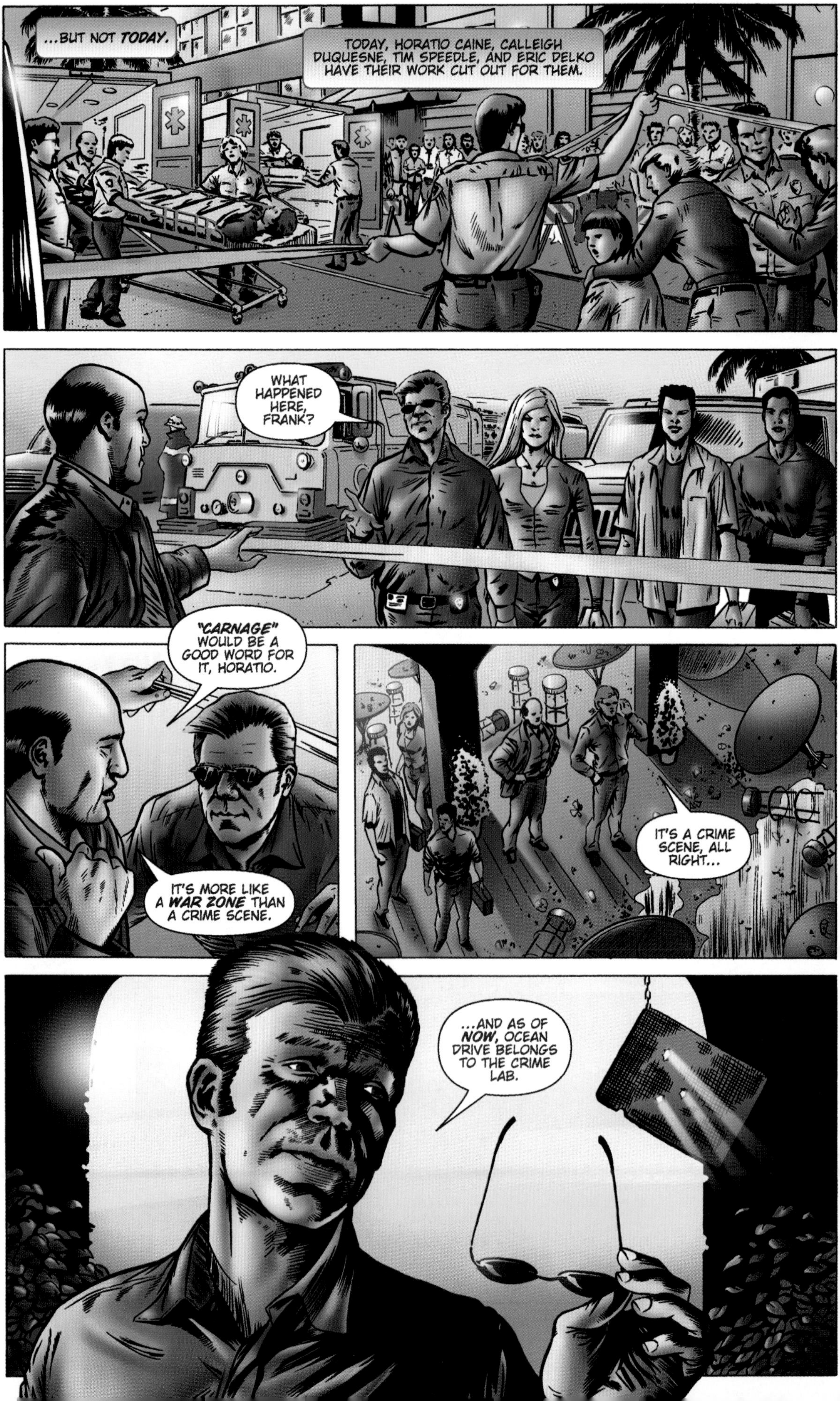
...BUT NOT *TODAY.*
TODAY, HORATIO CAINE, CALLEIGH DUQUESNE, TIM SPEEDLE, AND ERIC DELKO HAVE THEIR WORK CUT OUT FOR THEM.
WHAT HAPPENED HERE, FRANK?
"CARNAGE" WOULD BE A GOOD WORD FOR IT, HORATIO.
IT'S MORE LIKE A *WAR ZONE* THAN A CRIME SCENE.
IT'S A CRIME SCENE, ALL RIGHT...
...AND AS OF *NOW,* OCEAN DRIVE BELONGS TO THE CRIME LAB.

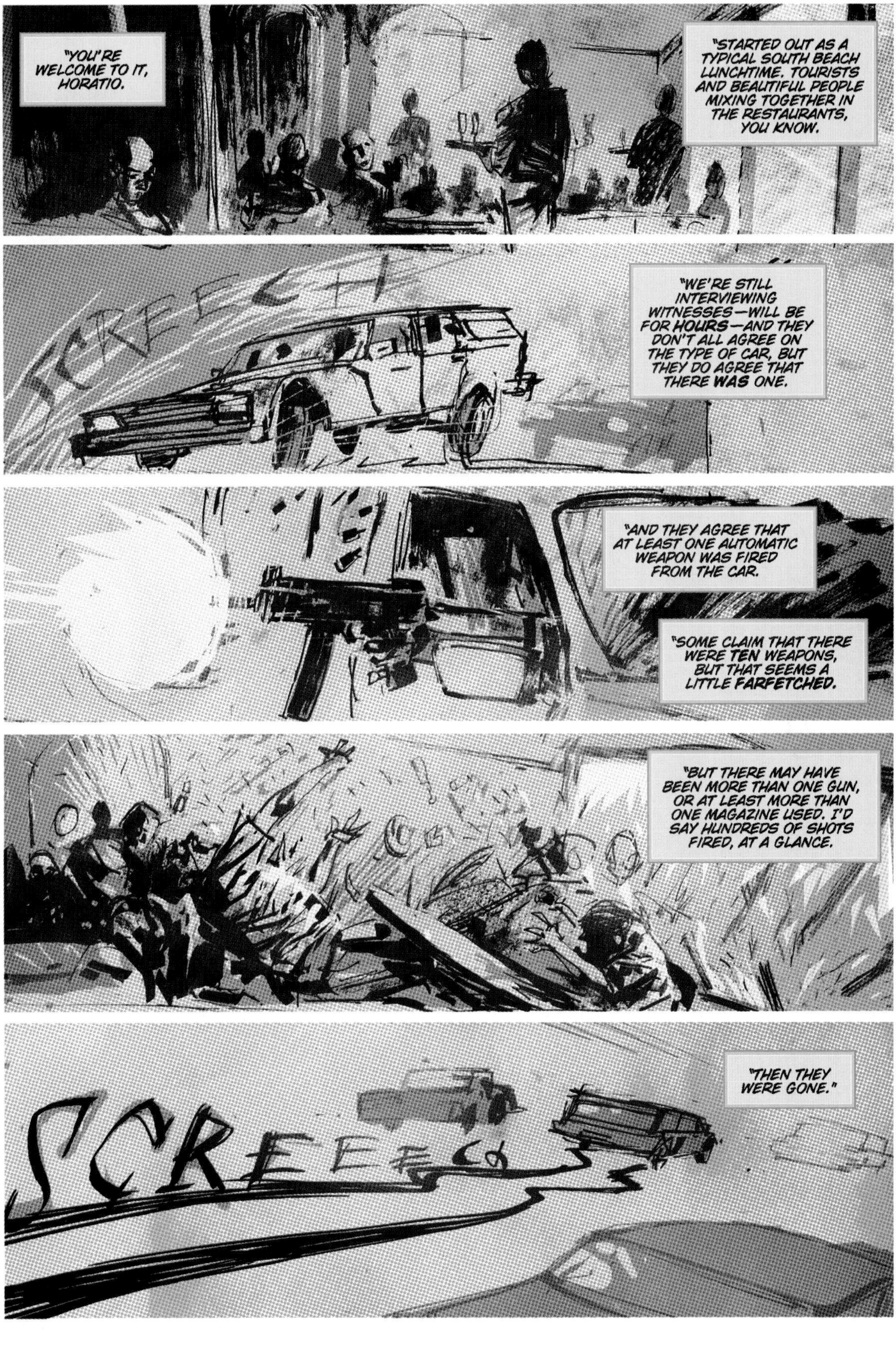
"YOU'RE WELCOME TO IT, HORATIO.
"STARTED OUT AS A TYPICAL SOUTH BEACH LUNCHTIME. TOURISTS AND BEAUTIFUL PEOPLE MIXING TOGETHER IN THE RESTAURANTS, YOU KNOW.
"WE'RE STILL INTERVIEWING WITNESSES—WILL BE FOR HOURS—AND THEY DON'T ALL AGREE ON THE TYPE OF CAR, BUT THEY DO AGREE THAT THERE WAS ONE.
"AND THEY AGREE THAT AT LEAST ONE AUTOMATIC WEAPON WAS FIRED FROM THE CAR.
"SOME CLAIM THAT THERE WERE TEN WEAPONS, BUT THAT SEEMS A LITTLE FARFETCHED.
"BUT THERE MAY HAVE BEEN MORE THAN ONE GUN, OR AT LEAST MORE THAN ONE MAGAZINE USED. I'D SAY HUNDREDS OF SHOTS FIRED, AT A GLANCE.
"THEN THEY WERE GONE."

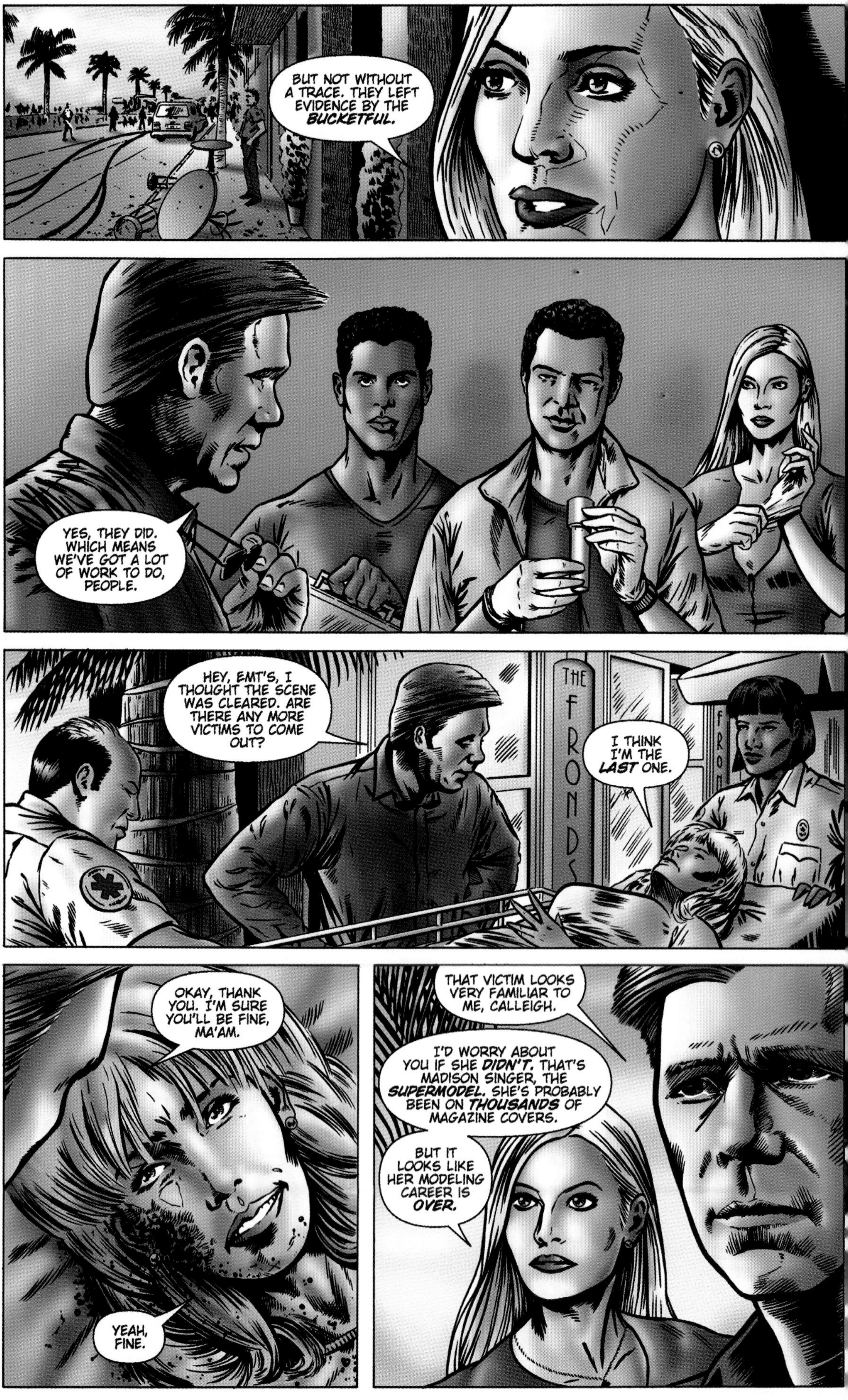
BUT NOT WITHOUT A TRACE. THEY LEFT EVIDENCE BY THE ***BUCKETFUL.***
YES, THEY DID. WHICH MEANS WE'VE GOT A LOT OF WORK TO DO, PEOPLE.
HEY, EMT'S, I THOUGHT THE SCENE WAS CLEARED. ARE THERE ANY MORE VICTIMS TO COME OUT?
THE FRONDS
I THINK I'M THE ***LAST*** ONE.
OKAY, THANK YOU. I'M SURE YOU'LL BE FINE, MA'AM.
YEAH, FINE.
THAT VICTIM LOOKS VERY FAMILIAR TO ME, CALLEIGH.
I'D WORRY ABOUT YOU IF SHE ***DIDN'T.*** THAT'S MADISON SINGER, THE ***SUPERMODEL.*** SHE'S PROBABLY BEEN ON ***THOUSANDS*** OF MAGAZINE COVERS.
BUT IT LOOKS LIKE HER MODELING CAREER IS ***OVER.***

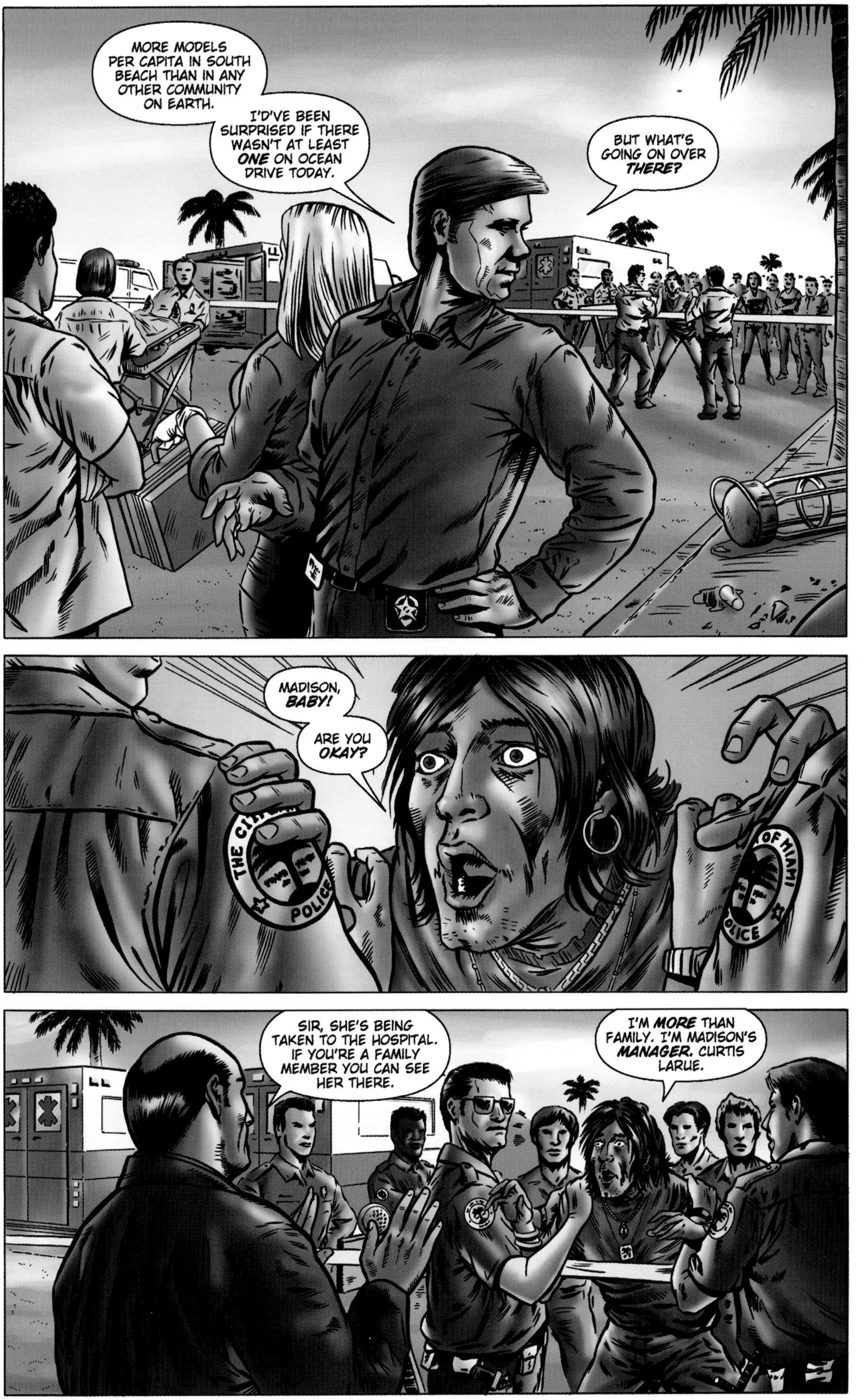
MORE MODELS PER CAPITA IN SOUTH BEACH THAN IN ANY OTHER COMMUNITY ON EARTH.
I'D'VE BEEN SURPRISED IF THERE WASN'T AT LEAST *ONE* ON OCEAN DRIVE TODAY.
BUT WHAT'S GOING ON OVER *THERE?*
MADISON, *BABY!*
ARE YOU *OKAY?*
THE CITY OF MIAMI POLICE
SIR, SHE'S BEING TAKEN TO THE HOSPITAL. IF YOU'RE A FAMILY MEMBER YOU CAN SEE HER THERE.
I'M *MORE* THAN FAMILY. I'M MADISON'S *MANAGER.* CURTIS LARUE.

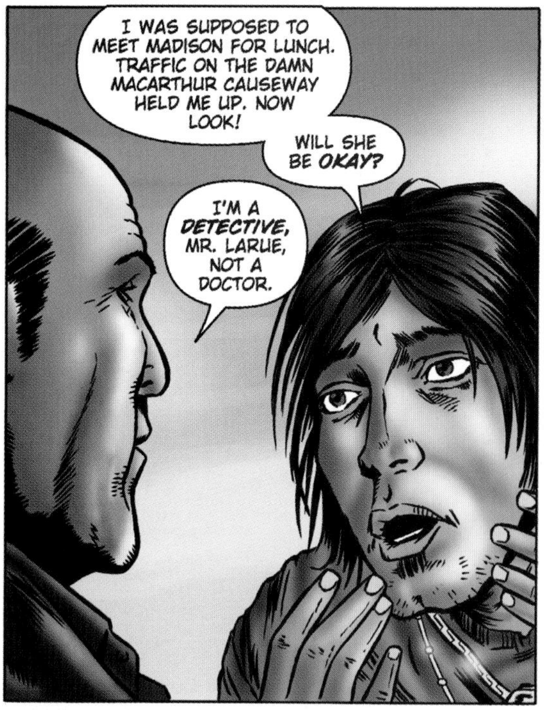
I WAS SUPPOSED TO MEET MADISON FOR LUNCH. TRAFFIC ON THE DAMN MACARTHUR CAUSEWAY HELD ME UP. NOW LOOK!
WILL SHE BE OKAY?
I'M A DETECTIVE, MR. LARUE, NOT A DOCTOR.

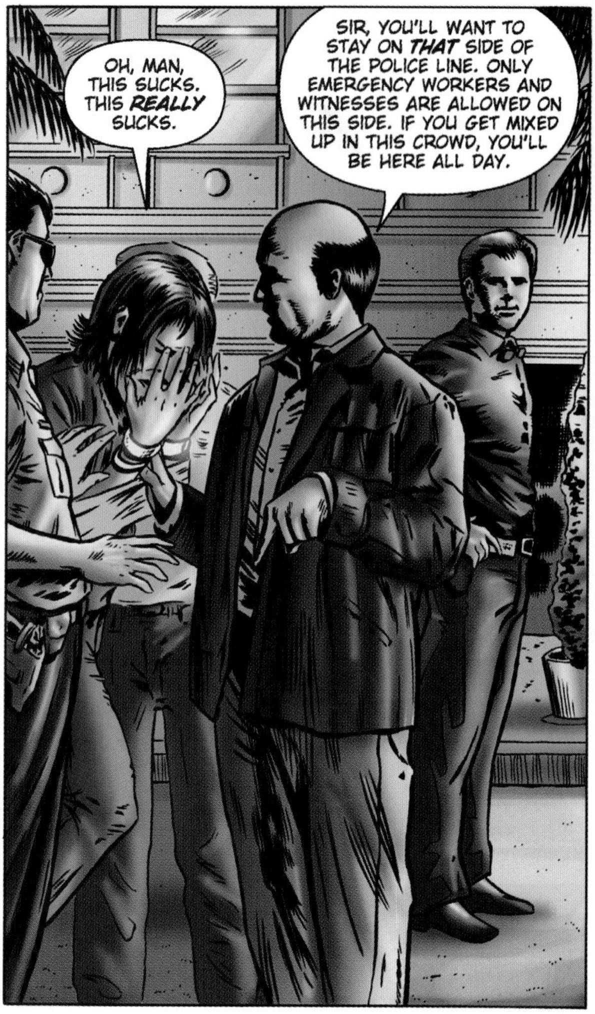
OH, MAN, THIS SUCKS. THIS REALLY SUCKS.
SIR, YOU'LL WANT TO STAY ON THAT SIDE OF THE POLICE LINE. ONLY EMERGENCY WORKERS AND WITNESSES ARE ALLOWED ON THIS SIDE. IF YOU GET MIXED UP IN THIS CROWD, YOU'LL BE HERE ALL DAY.

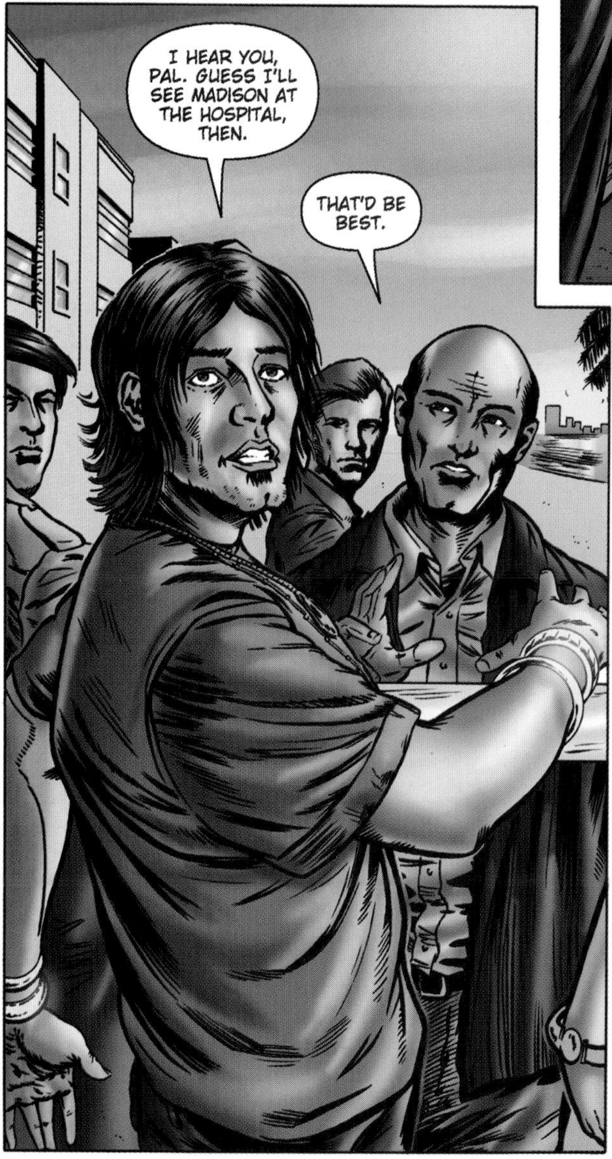
I HEAR YOU, PAL. GUESS I'LL SEE MADISON AT THE HOSPITAL, THEN.
THAT'D BE BEST.

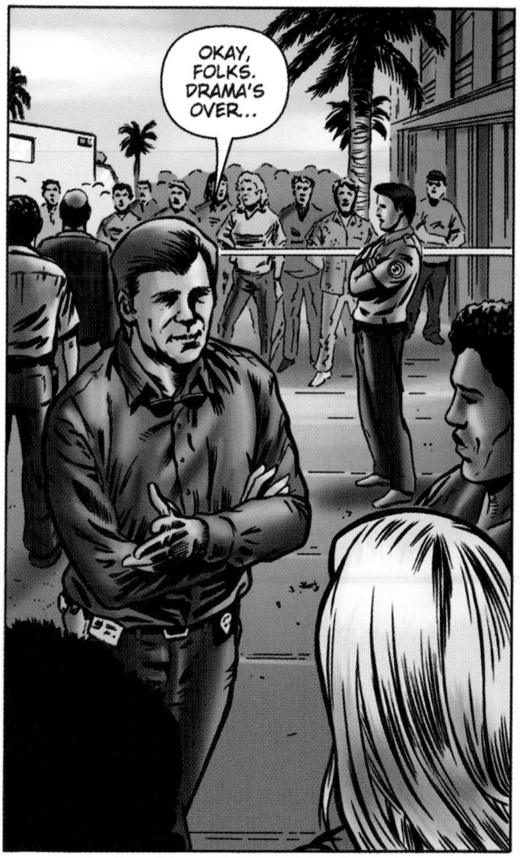
OKAY, FOLKS. DRAMA'S OVER...

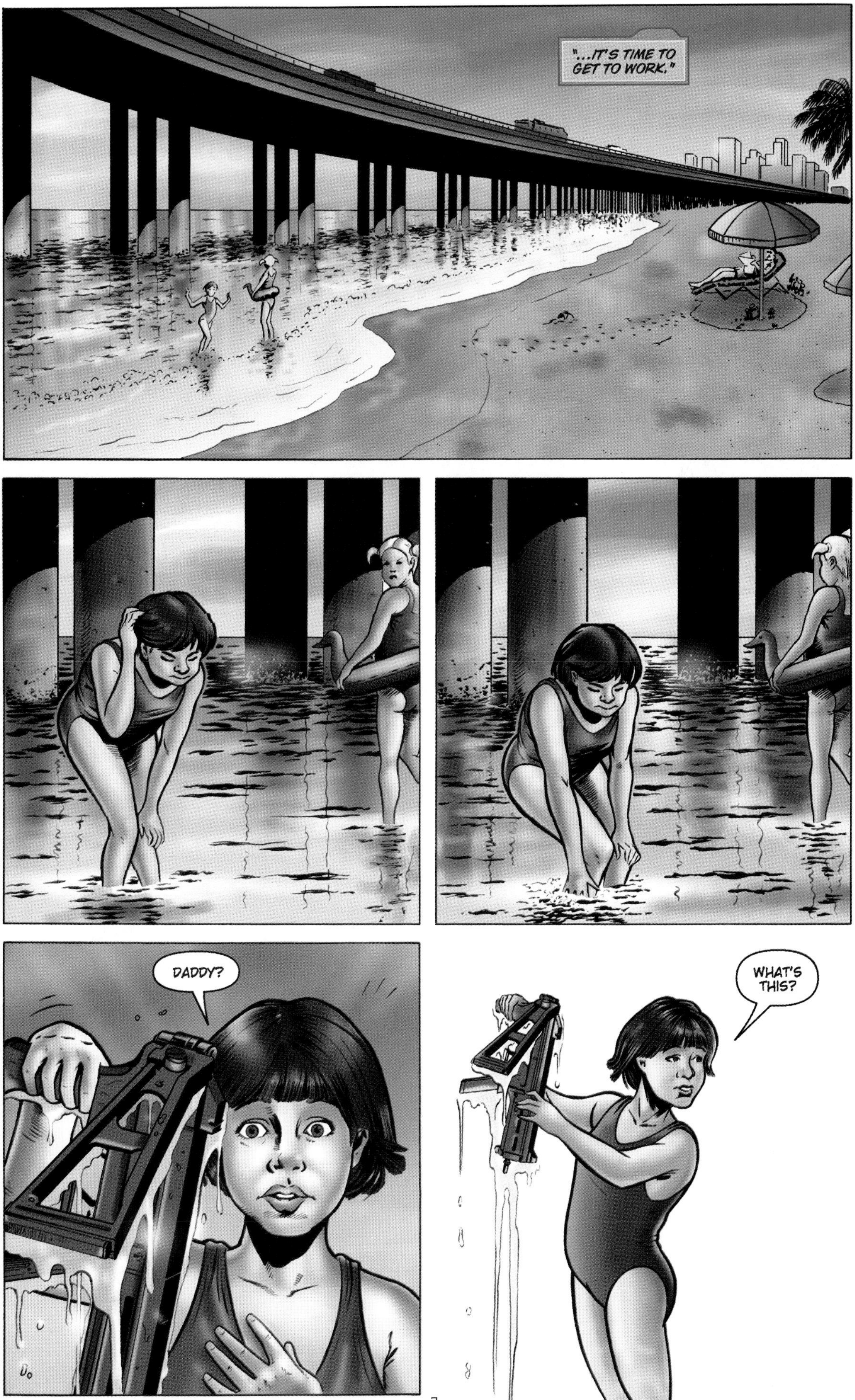
"...IT'S TIME TO GET TO WORK."
DADDY?
WHAT'S THIS?

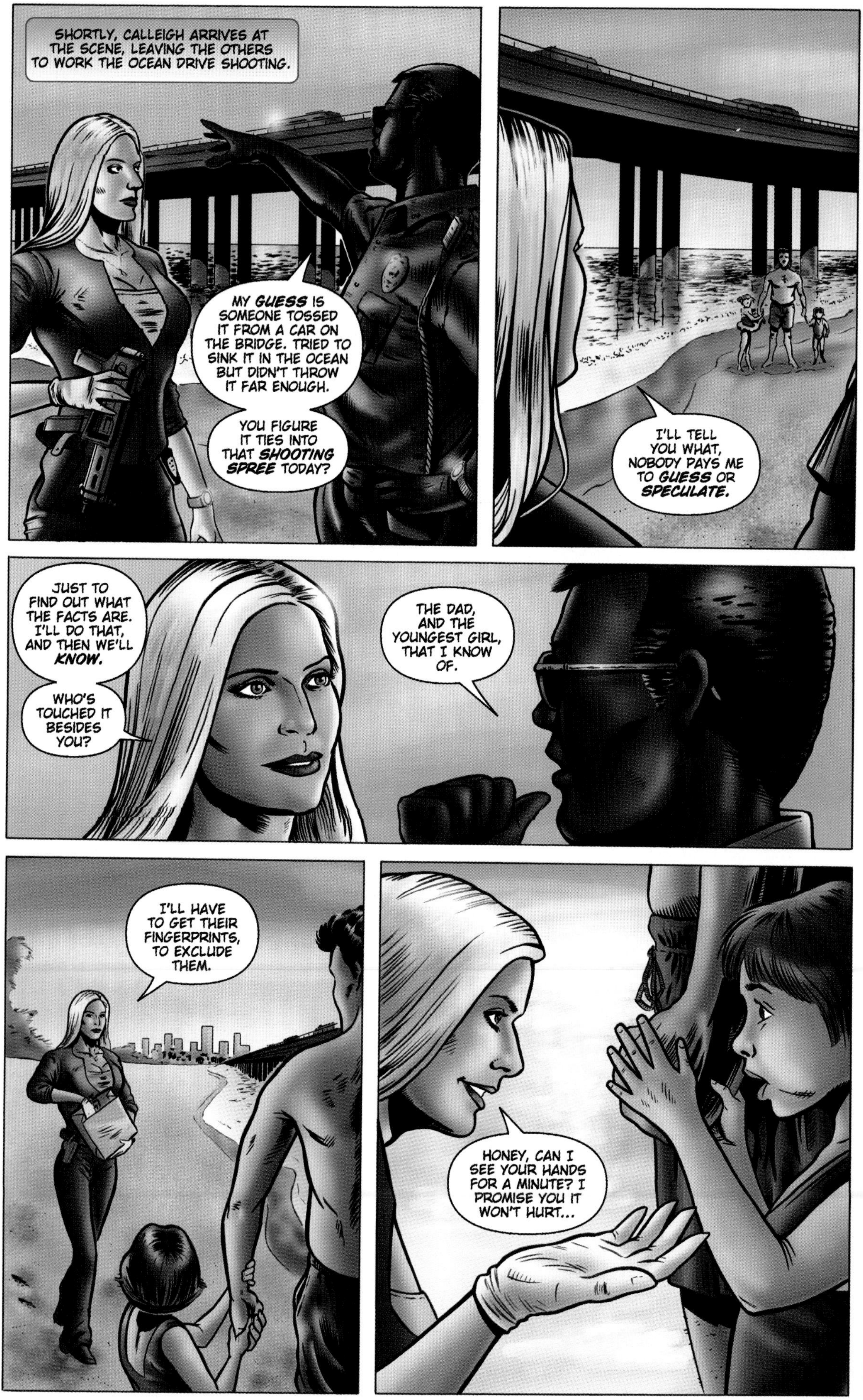
SHORTLY, CALLEIGH ARRIVES AT THE SCENE, LEAVING THE OTHERS TO WORK THE OCEAN DRIVE SHOOTING.
MY GUESS IS SOMEONE TOSSED IT FROM A CAR ON THE BRIDGE. TRIED TO SINK IT IN THE OCEAN BUT DIDN'T THROW IT FAR ENOUGH.
YOU FIGURE IT TIES INTO THAT SHOOTING SPREE TODAY?
I'LL TELL YOU WHAT, NOBODY PAYS ME TO GUESS OR SPECULATE.
JUST TO FIND OUT WHAT THE FACTS ARE. I'LL DO THAT, AND THEN WE'LL KNOW.
WHO'S TOUCHED IT BESIDES YOU?
THE DAD, AND THE YOUNGEST GIRL, THAT I KNOW OF.
I'LL HAVE TO GET THEIR FINGERPRINTS, TO EXCLUDE THEM.
HONEY, CAN I SEE YOUR HANDS FOR A MINUTE? I PROMISE YOU IT WON'T HURT...

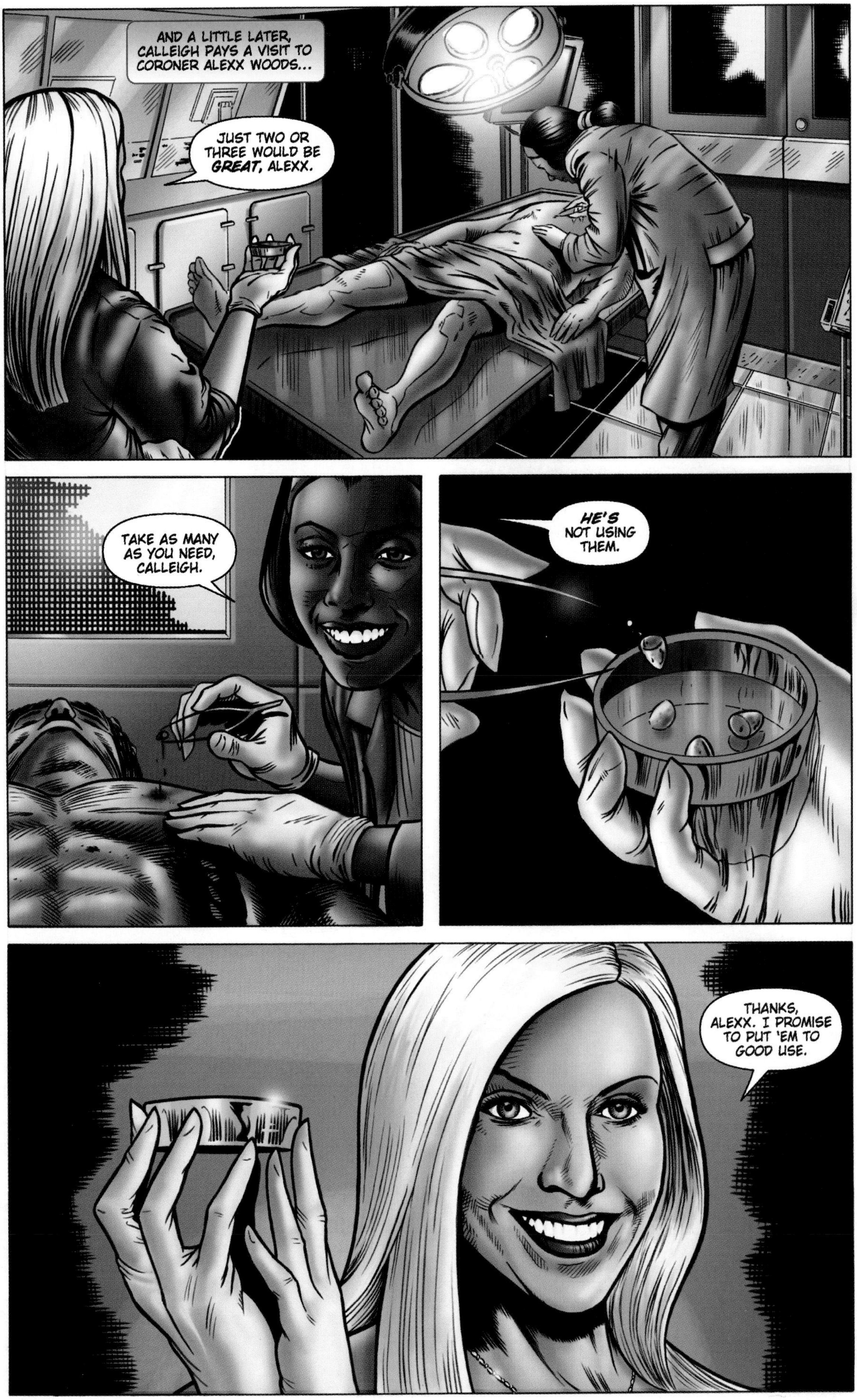
AND A LITTLE LATER, CALLEIGH PAYS A VISIT TO CORONER ALEXX WOODS...
JUST TWO OR THREE WOULD BE GREAT, ALEXX.
TAKE AS MANY AS YOU NEED, CALLEIGH.
HE'S NOT USING THEM.
THANKS, ALEXX. I PROMISE TO PUT 'EM TO GOOD USE.

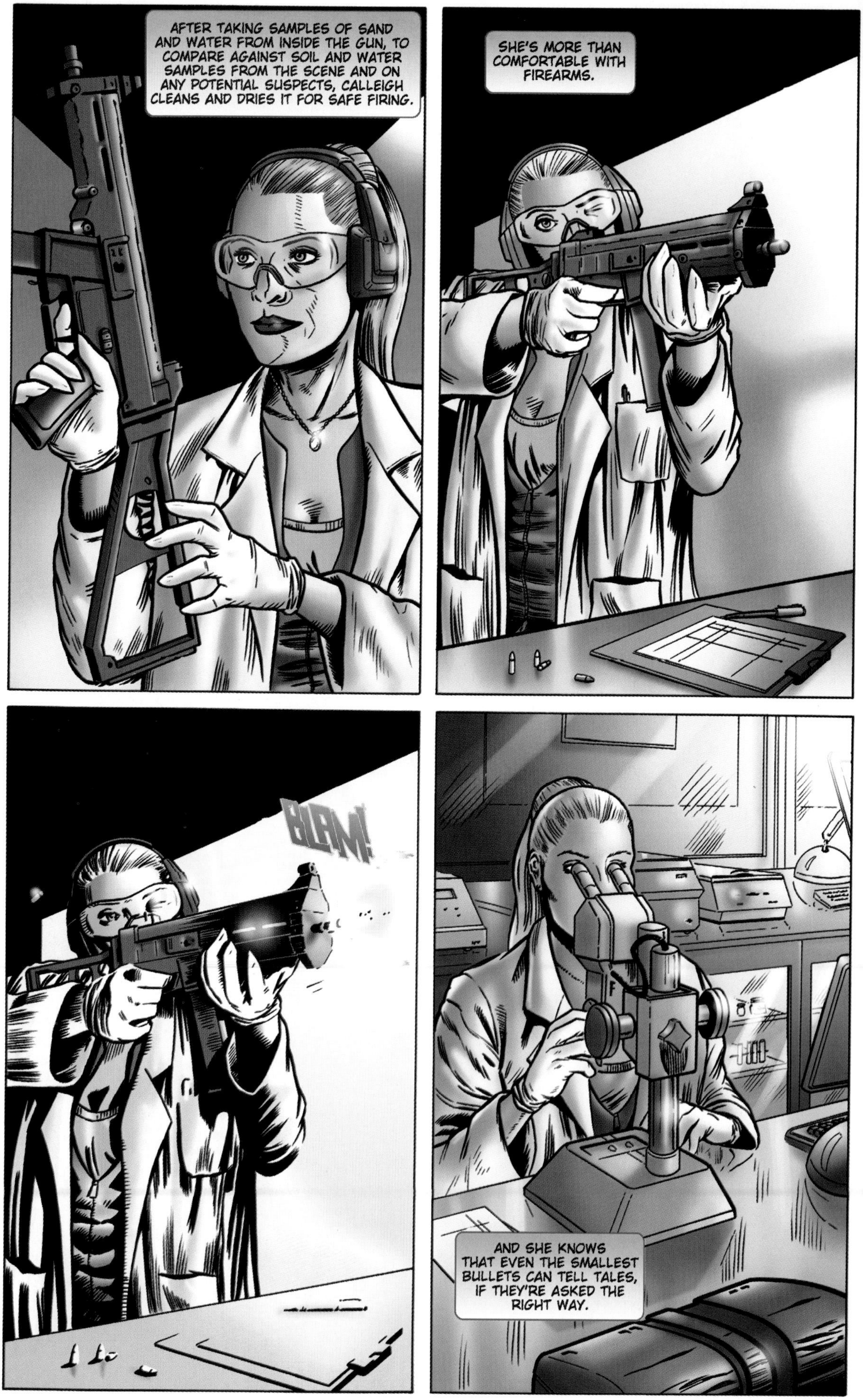
AFTER TAKING SAMPLES OF SAND AND WATER FROM INSIDE THE GUN, TO COMPARE AGAINST SOIL AND WATER SAMPLES FROM THE SCENE AND ON ANY POTENTIAL SUSPECTS, CALLEIGH CLEANS AND DRIES IT FOR SAFE FIRING.
SHE'S MORE THAN COMFORTABLE WITH FIREARMS.
BLAM!
AND SHE KNOWS THAT EVEN THE SMALLEST BULLETS CAN TELL TALES, IF THEY'RE ASKED THE RIGHT WAY.

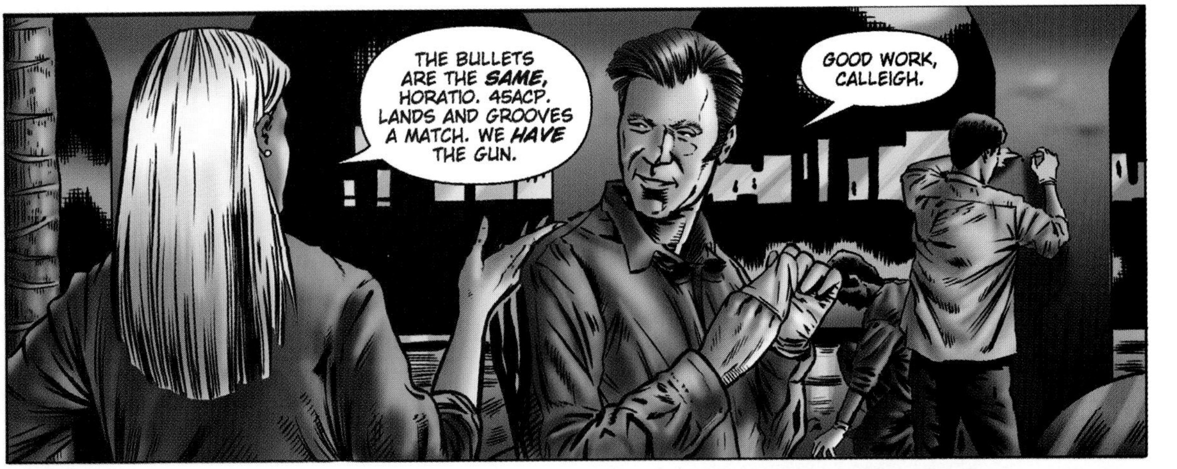
THE BULLETS ARE THE SAME, HORATIO. 45ACP. LANDS AND GROOVES A MATCH. WE HAVE THE GUN.
GOOD WORK, CALLEIGH.

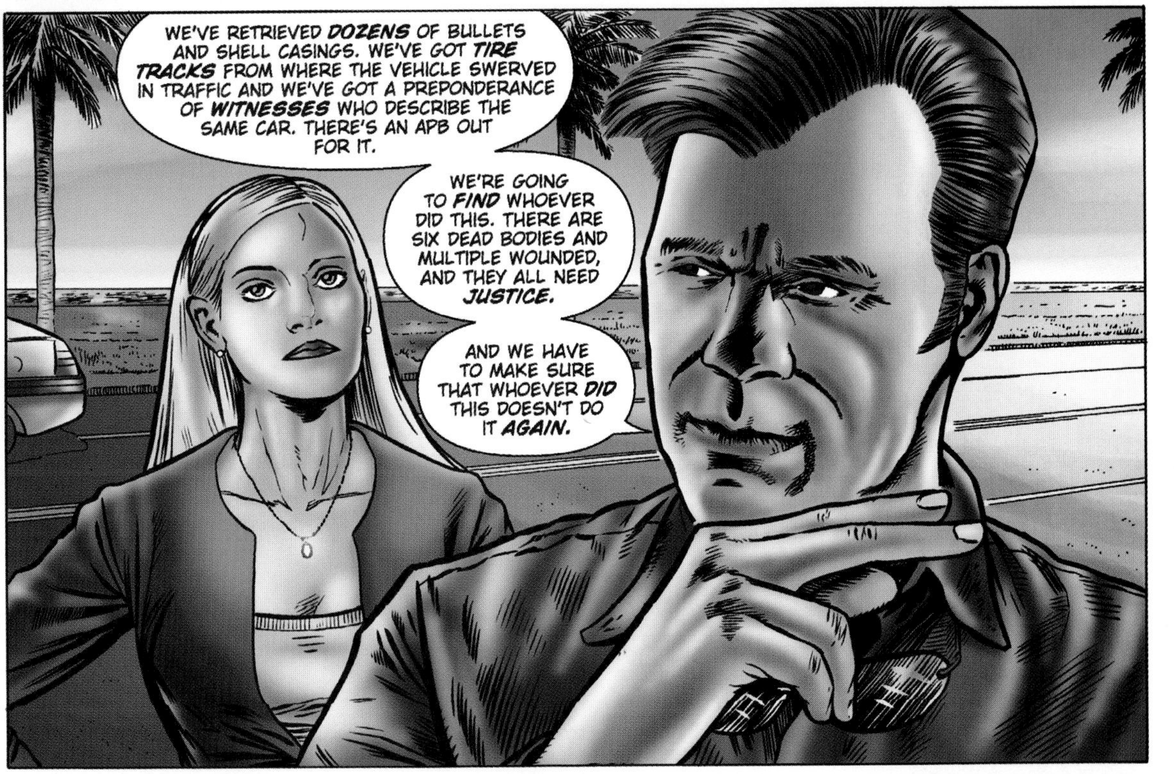
WE'VE RETRIEVED DOZENS OF BULLETS AND SHELL CASINGS. WE'VE GOT TIRE TRACKS FROM WHERE THE VEHICLE SWERVED IN TRAFFIC AND WE'VE GOT A PREPONDERANCE OF WITNESSES WHO DESCRIBE THE SAME CAR. THERE'S AN APB OUT FOR IT.
WE'RE GOING TO FIND WHOEVER DID THIS. THERE ARE SIX DEAD BODIES AND MULTIPLE WOUNDED, AND THEY ALL NEED JUSTICE.
AND WE HAVE TO MAKE SURE THAT WHOEVER DID THIS DOESN'T DO IT AGAIN.

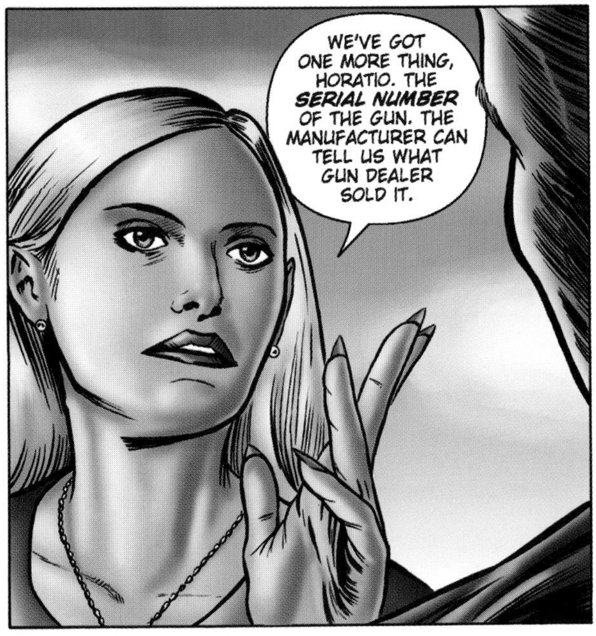
WE'VE GOT ONE MORE THING, HORATIO. THE SERIAL NUMBER OF THE GUN. THE MANUFACTURER CAN TELL US WHAT GUN DEALER SOLD IT.

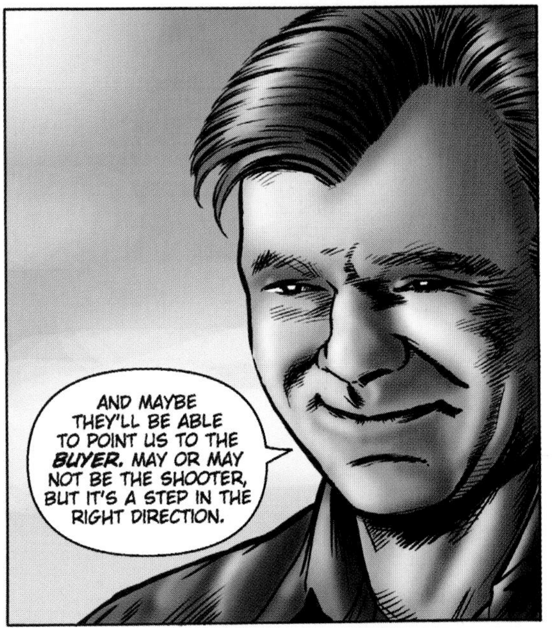
AND MAYBE THEY'LL BE ABLE TO POINT US TO THE BUYER. MAY OR MAY NOT BE THE SHOOTER, BUT IT'S A STEP IN THE RIGHT DIRECTION.

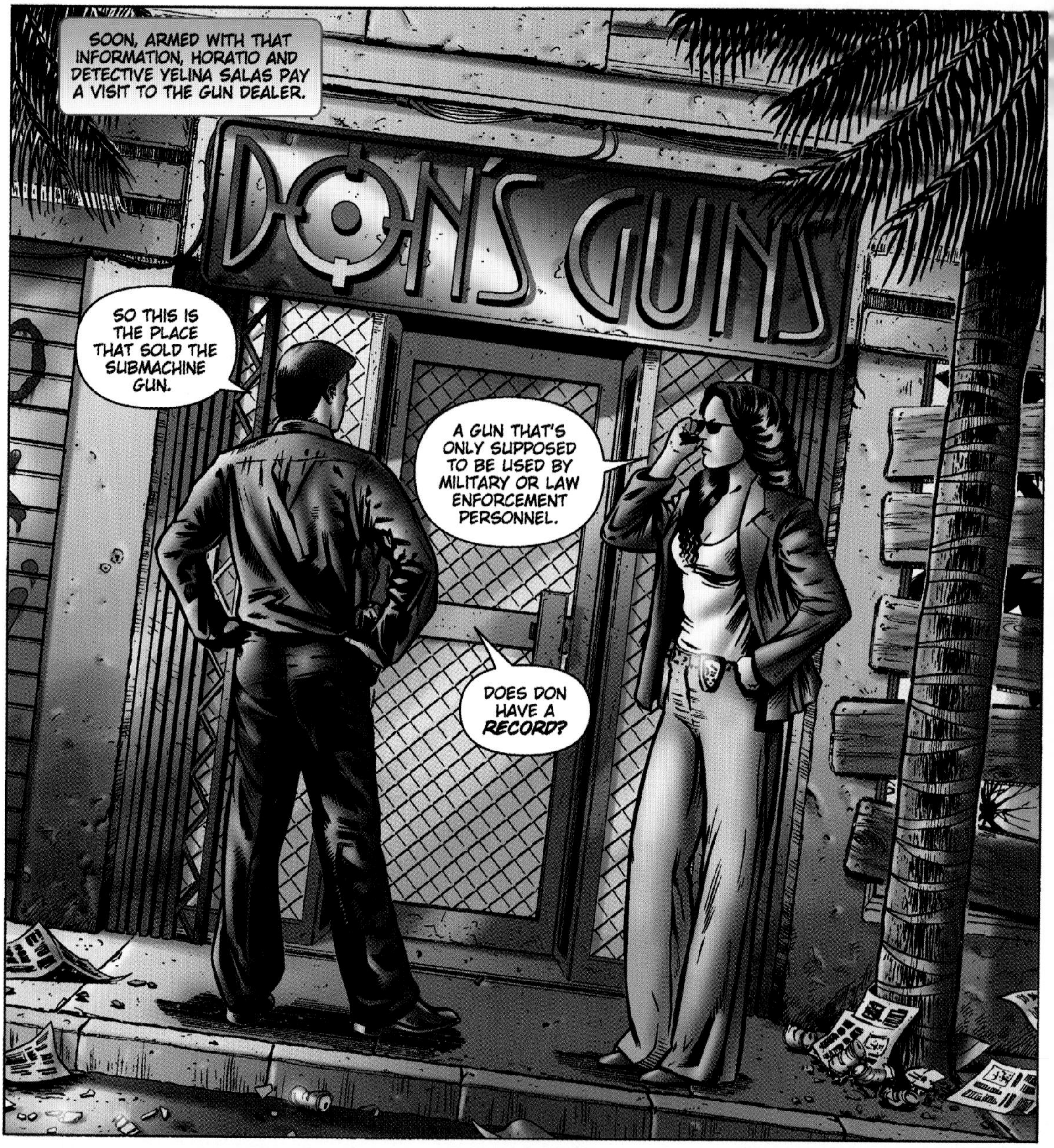
SOON, ARMED WITH THAT INFORMATION, HORATIO AND DETECTIVE YELINA SALAS PAY A VISIT TO THE GUN DEALER.
DON'S GUNS
SO THIS IS THE PLACE THAT SOLD THE SUBMACHINE GUN.
A GUN THAT'S ONLY SUPPOSED TO BE USED BY MILITARY OR LAW ENFORCEMENT PERSONNEL.
DOES DON HAVE A *RECORD?*

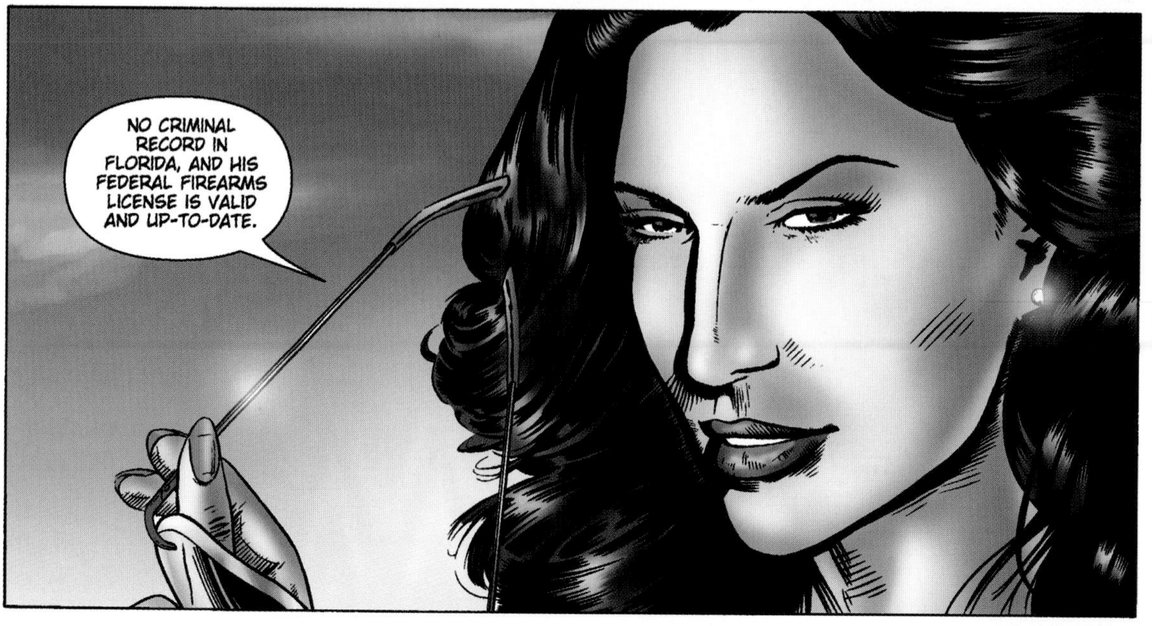
NO CRIMINAL RECORD IN FLORIDA, AND HIS FEDERAL FIREARMS LICENSE IS VALID AND UP-TO-DATE.

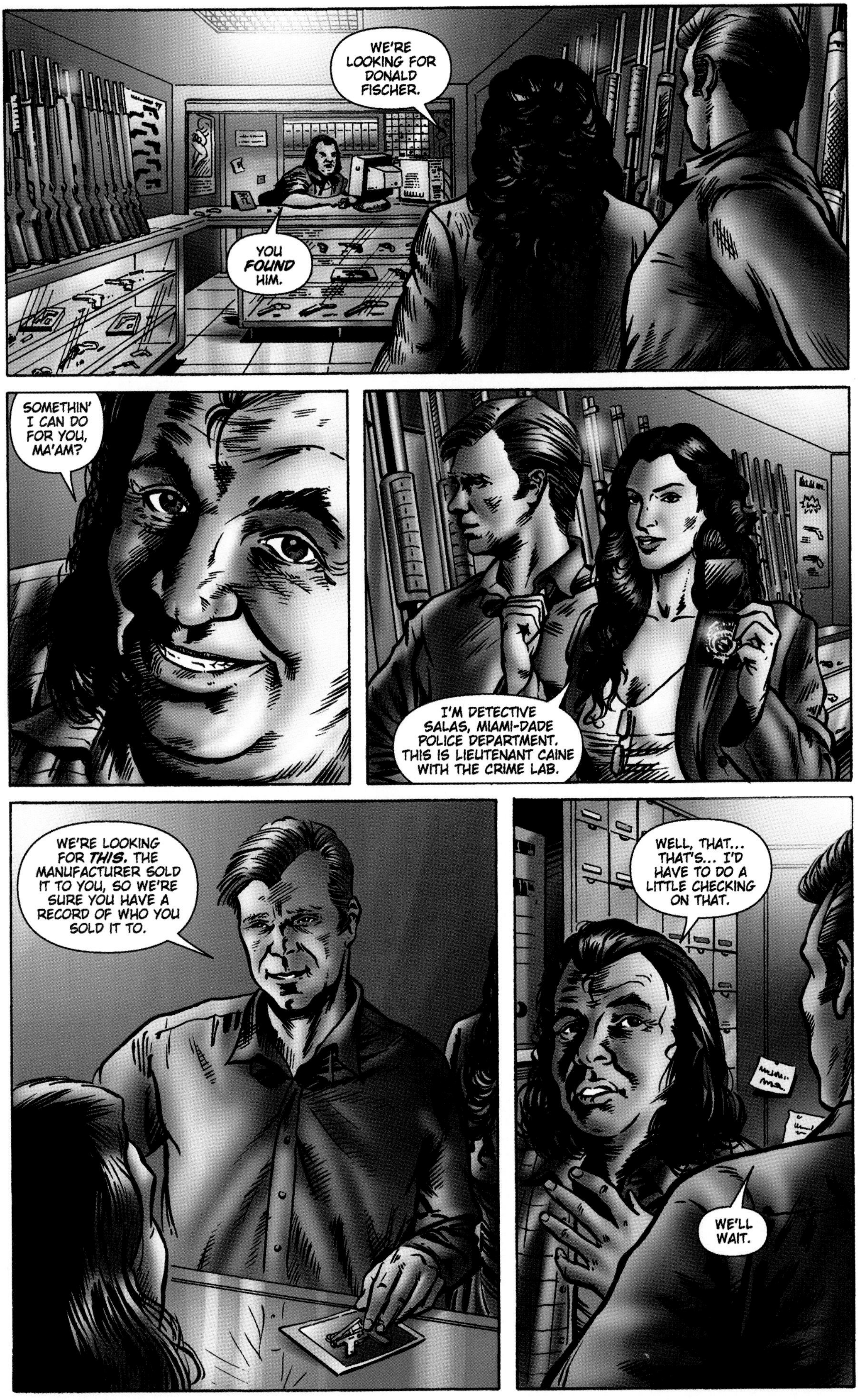
WE'RE LOOKING FOR DONALD FISCHER.
YOU FOUND HIM.
SOMETHIN' I CAN DO FOR YOU, MA'AM?
I'M DETECTIVE SALAS, MIAMI-DADE POLICE DEPARTMENT. THIS IS LIEUTENANT CAINE WITH THE CRIME LAB.
WE'RE LOOKING FOR THIS. THE MANUFACTURER SOLD IT TO YOU, SO WE'RE SURE YOU HAVE A RECORD OF WHO YOU SOLD IT TO.
WELL, THAT... THAT'S... I'D HAVE TO DO A LITTLE CHECKING ON THAT.
WE'LL WAIT.

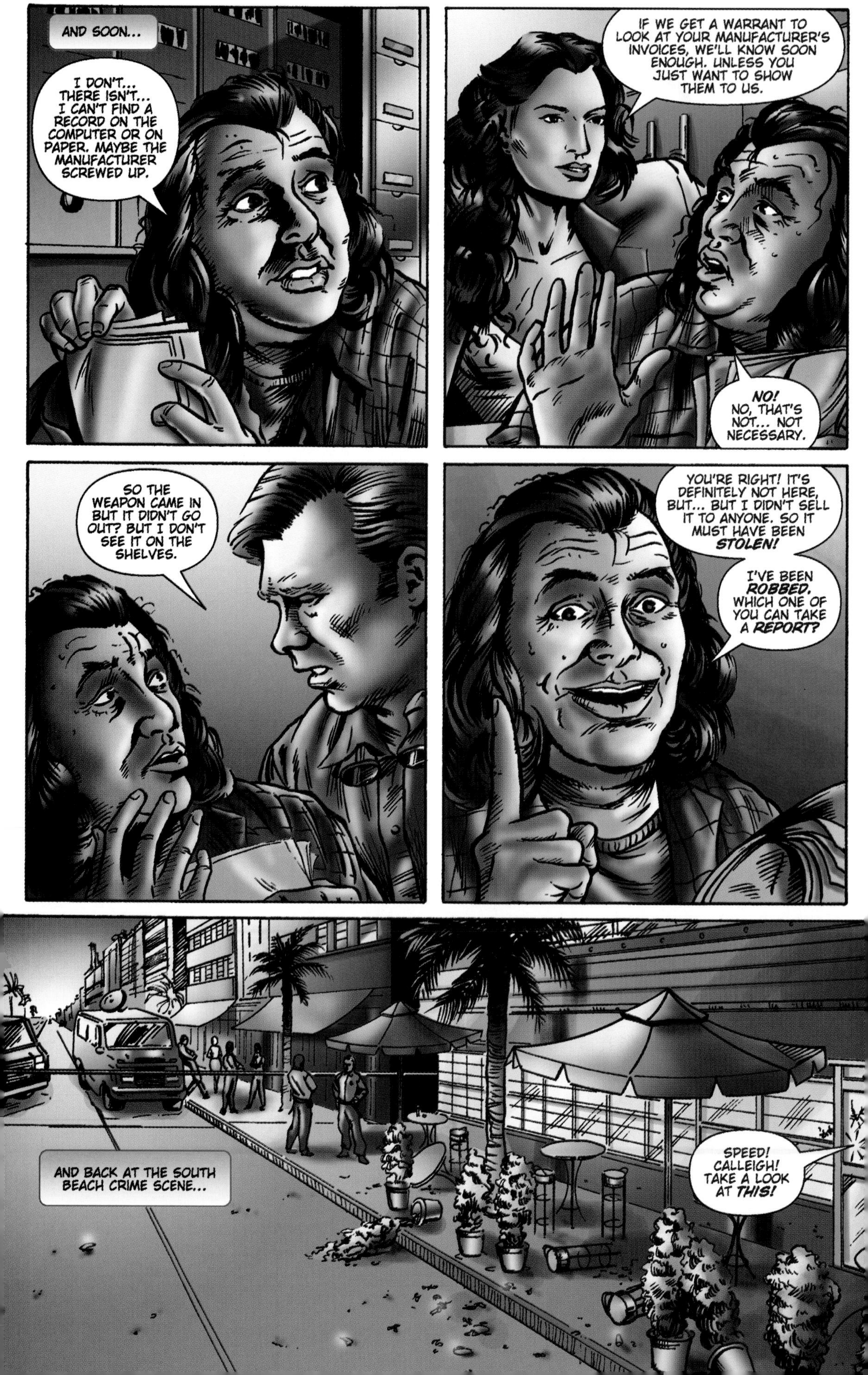
AND SOON...
I DON'T... THERE ISN'T... I CAN'T FIND A RECORD ON THE COMPUTER OR ON PAPER. MAYBE THE MANUFACTURER SCREWED UP.
IF WE GET A WARRANT TO LOOK AT YOUR MANUFACTURER'S INVOICES, WE'LL KNOW SOON ENOUGH. UNLESS YOU JUST WANT TO SHOW THEM TO US.
NO! NO, THAT'S NOT... NOT NECESSARY.
SO THE WEAPON CAME IN BUT IT DIDN'T GO OUT? BUT I DON'T SEE IT ON THE SHELVES.
YOU'RE RIGHT! IT'S DEFINITELY NOT HERE, BUT... BUT I DIDN'T SELL IT TO ANYONE. SO IT MUST HAVE BEEN STOLEN!
I'VE BEEN ROBBED. WHICH ONE OF YOU CAN TAKE A REPORT?
AND BACK AT THE SOUTH BEACH CRIME SCENE...
SPEED! CALLEIGH! TAKE A LOOK AT THIS!

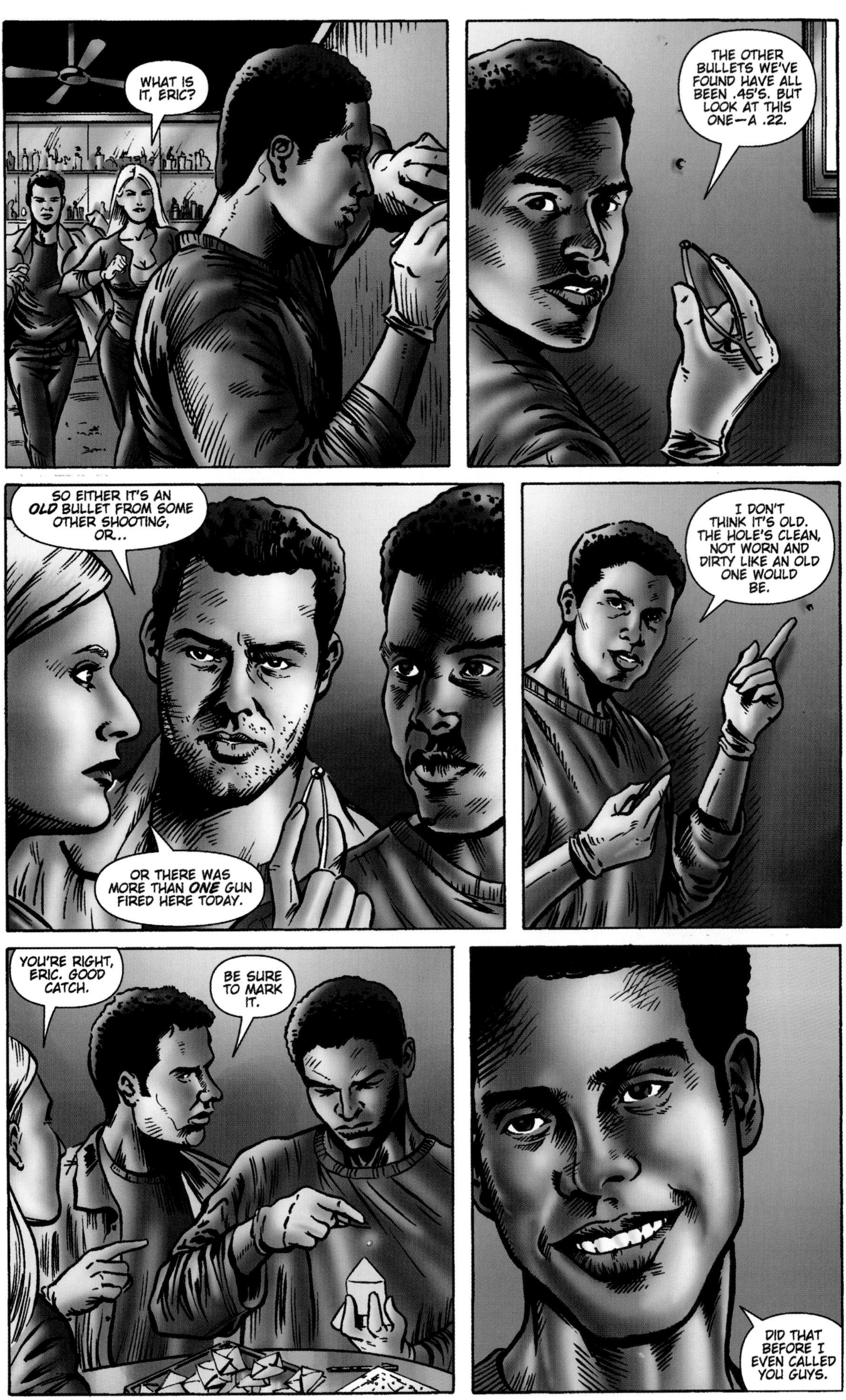
WHAT IS IT, ERIC?
THE OTHER BULLETS WE'VE FOUND HAVE ALL BEEN .45'S. BUT LOOK AT THIS ONE—A .22.
SO EITHER IT'S AN OLD BULLET FROM SOME OTHER SHOOTING, OR..
OR THERE WAS MORE THAN ONE GUN FIRED HERE TODAY.
I DON'T THINK IT'S OLD. THE HOLE'S CLEAN, NOT WORN AND DIRTY LIKE AN OLD ONE WOULD BE.
YOU'RE RIGHT, ERIC. GOOD CATCH.
BE SURE TO MARK IT.
DID THAT BEFORE I EVEN CALLED YOU GUYS.

"SHE'S STILL HEAVILY SEDATED, LT. CAINE."

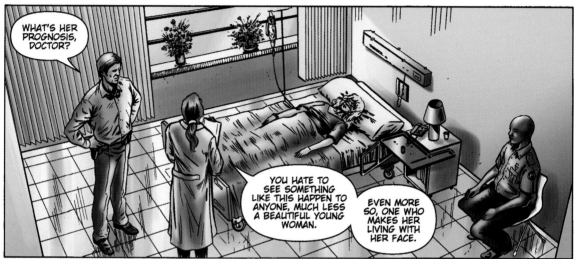

WHAT'S HER PROGNOSIS, DOCTOR?

YOU HATE TO SEE SOMETHING LIKE THIS HAPPEN TO ANYONE, MUCH LESS A BEAUTIFUL YOUNG WOMAN.

EVEN MORE SO, ONE WHO MAKES HER LIVING WITH HER FACE.

HER LIFE ISN'T IN DANGER. BUT SHE'LL NEED A *LOT* OF RECONSTRUCTIVE SURGERY BEFORE HER FACE WILL EVEN BEGIN TO LOOK THE SAME.

I DOUBT THAT SHE'LL EVER GET HER LOOKS BACK COMPLETELY.

SHE'S NOT... A *SUSPECT* IN ANYTHING, IS SHE?

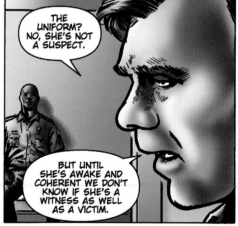

THE UNIFORM? NO, SHE'S NOT A SUSPECT.

BUT UNTIL SHE'S AWAKE AND COHERENT WE DON'T KNOW IF SHE'S A WITNESS AS WELL AS A VICTIM.

THAT'S THE BOYFRIEND. JOEL SUTPHEN. HE'S BEEN HERE MOST OF THE DAY. I'VE TRIED TO GET HIM TO GO EAT A MEAL, TAKE A NAP, SOMETHING. BUT HE'S DEVOTED.

YOU'VE SEEN HER. DO YOU BLAME HIM?

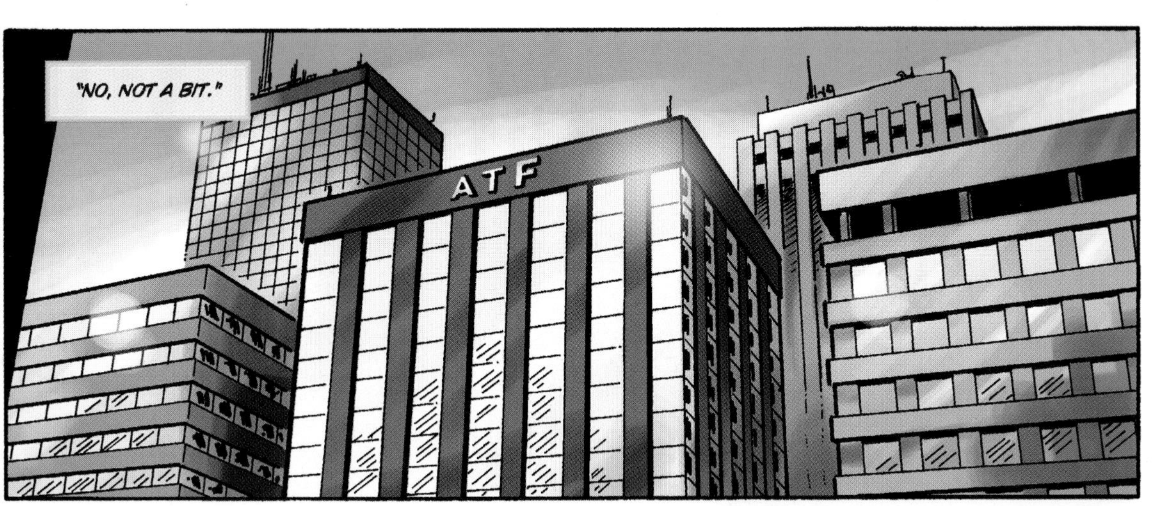
"NO, NOT A BIT."
ATF

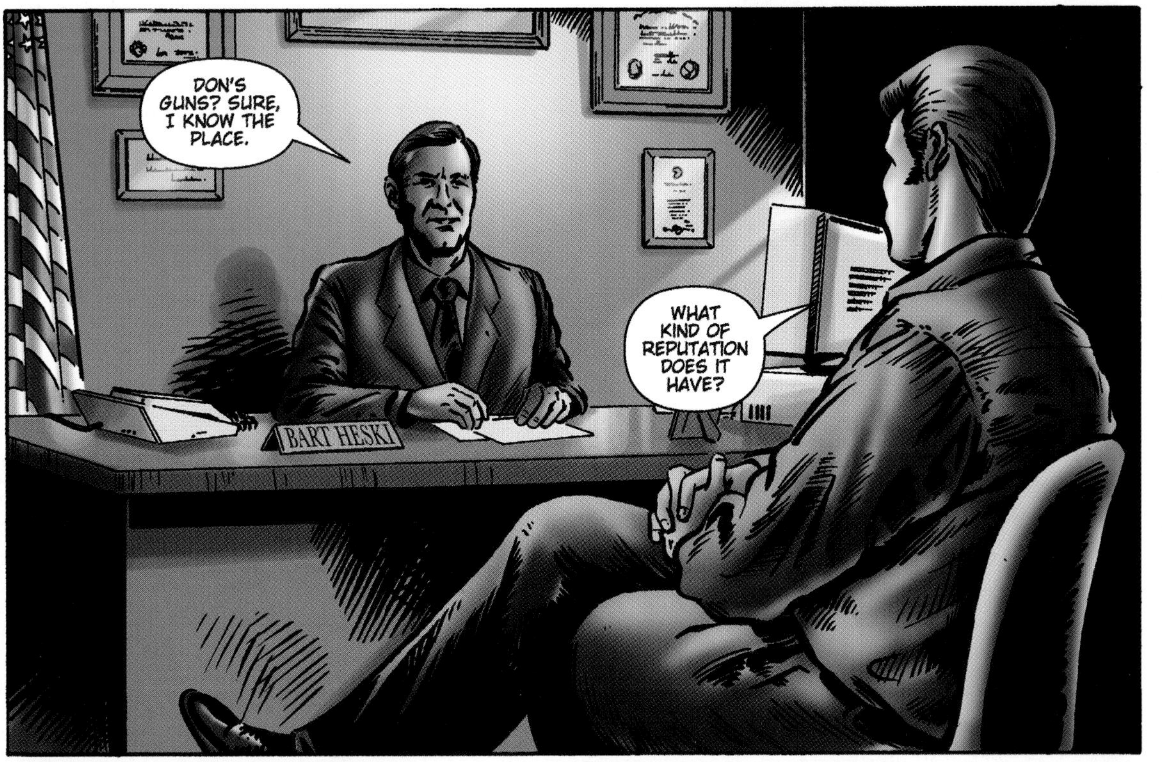
DON'S GUNS? SURE, I KNOW THE PLACE.
WHAT KIND OF REPUTATION DOES IT HAVE?
BART HESKI

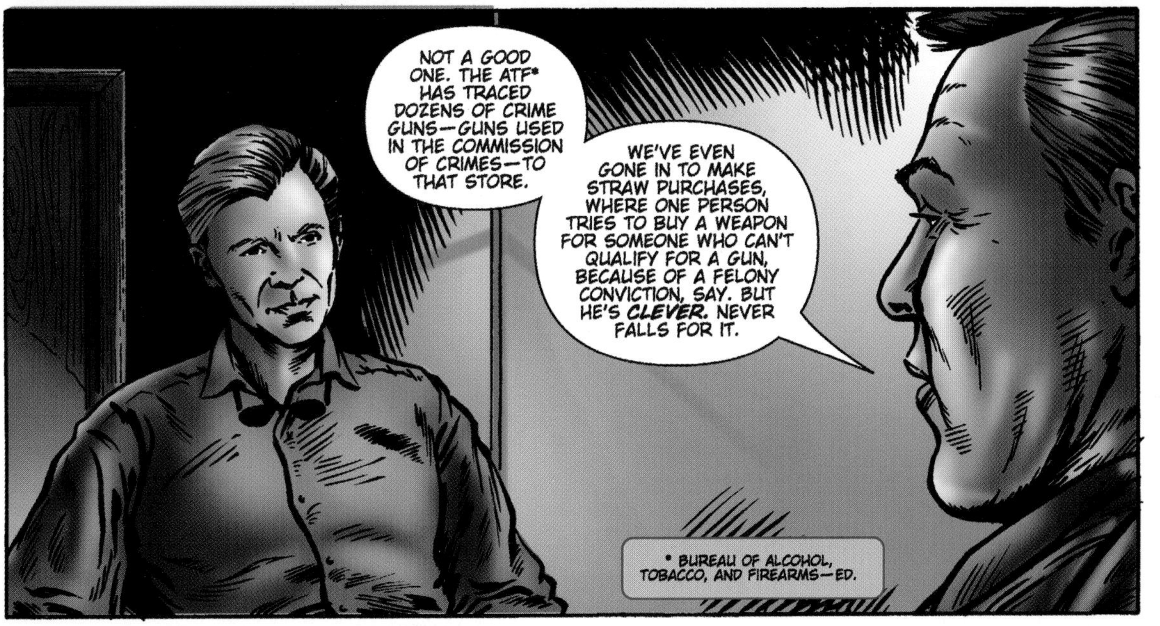
NOT A GOOD ONE. THE ATF* HAS TRACED DOZENS OF CRIME GUNS—GUNS USED IN THE COMMISSION OF CRIMES—TO THAT STORE.
WE'VE EVEN GONE IN TO MAKE STRAW PURCHASES, WHERE ONE PERSON TRIES TO BUY A WEAPON FOR SOMEONE WHO CAN'T QUALIFY FOR A GUN, BECAUSE OF A FELONY CONVICTION, SAY. BUT HE'S *CLEVER.* NEVER FALLS FOR IT.
* BUREAU OF ALCOHOL, TOBACCO, AND FIREARMS—ED.

SO MAYBE HE'S *CLEAN?*

I DON'T THINK SO. I JUST THINK HE'S CAREFUL.

SOMEHOW, THOUGH, HE'S SUPPLYING WEAPONS TO CRIMINALS.

IF YOU *KNOW* THAT, WHY HAVEN'T YOU BUSTED HIM?

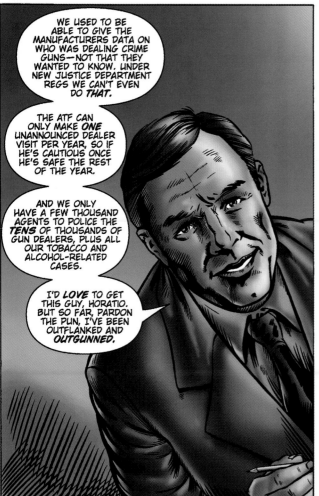

WE USED TO BE ABLE TO GIVE THE MANUFACTURERS DATA ON WHO WAS DEALING CRIME GUNS—NOT THAT THEY WANTED TO KNOW. UNDER NEW JUSTICE DEPARTMENT REGS WE CAN'T EVEN DO *THAT.*

THE ATF CAN ONLY MAKE *ONE* UNANNOUNCED DEALER VISIT PER YEAR, SO IF HE'S CAUTIOUS ONCE HE'S SAFE THE REST OF THE YEAR.

AND WE ONLY HAVE A FEW THOUSAND AGENTS TO POLICE THE *TENS* OF THOUSANDS OF GUN DEALERS, PLUS ALL OUR TOBACCO AND ALCOHOL-RELATED CASES.

I'D *LOVE* TO GET THIS GUY, HORATIO. BUT SO FAR, PARDON THE PUN, I'VE BEEN OUTFLANKED AND *OUTGUNNED.*

WELL, BART, MAYBE I CAN *HELP.*

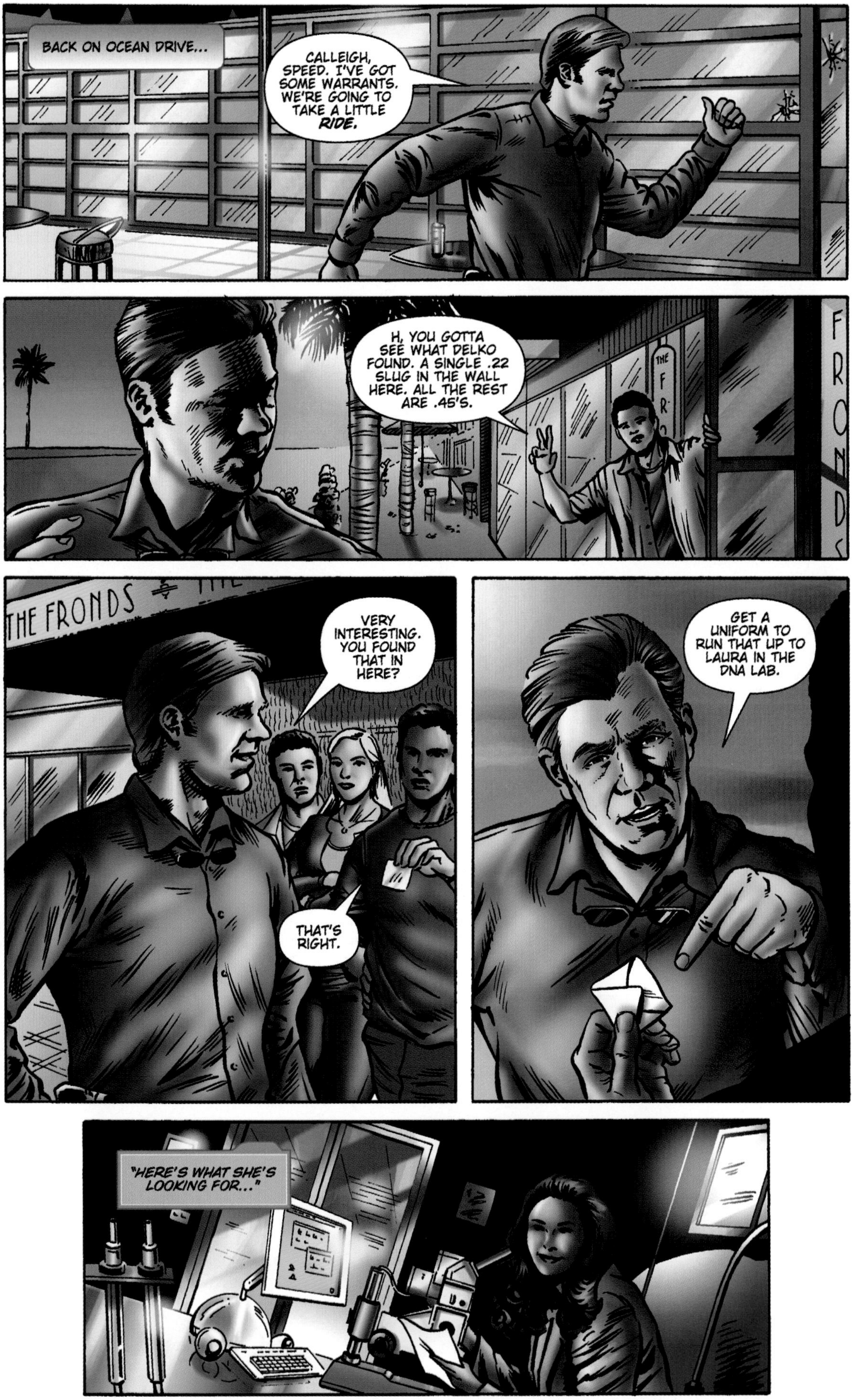
BACK ON OCEAN DRIVE...
CALLEIGH, SPEED. I'VE GOT SOME WARRANTS. WE'RE GOING TO TAKE A LITTLE RIDE.
H, YOU GOTTA SEE WHAT DELKO FOUND. A SINGLE .22 SLUG IN THE WALL HERE. ALL THE REST ARE .45'S.
THE FRONDS
VERY INTERESTING. YOU FOUND THAT IN HERE?
THAT'S RIGHT.
GET A UNIFORM TO RUN THAT UP TO LAURA IN THE DNA LAB.
"HERE'S WHAT SHE'S LOOKING FOR..."

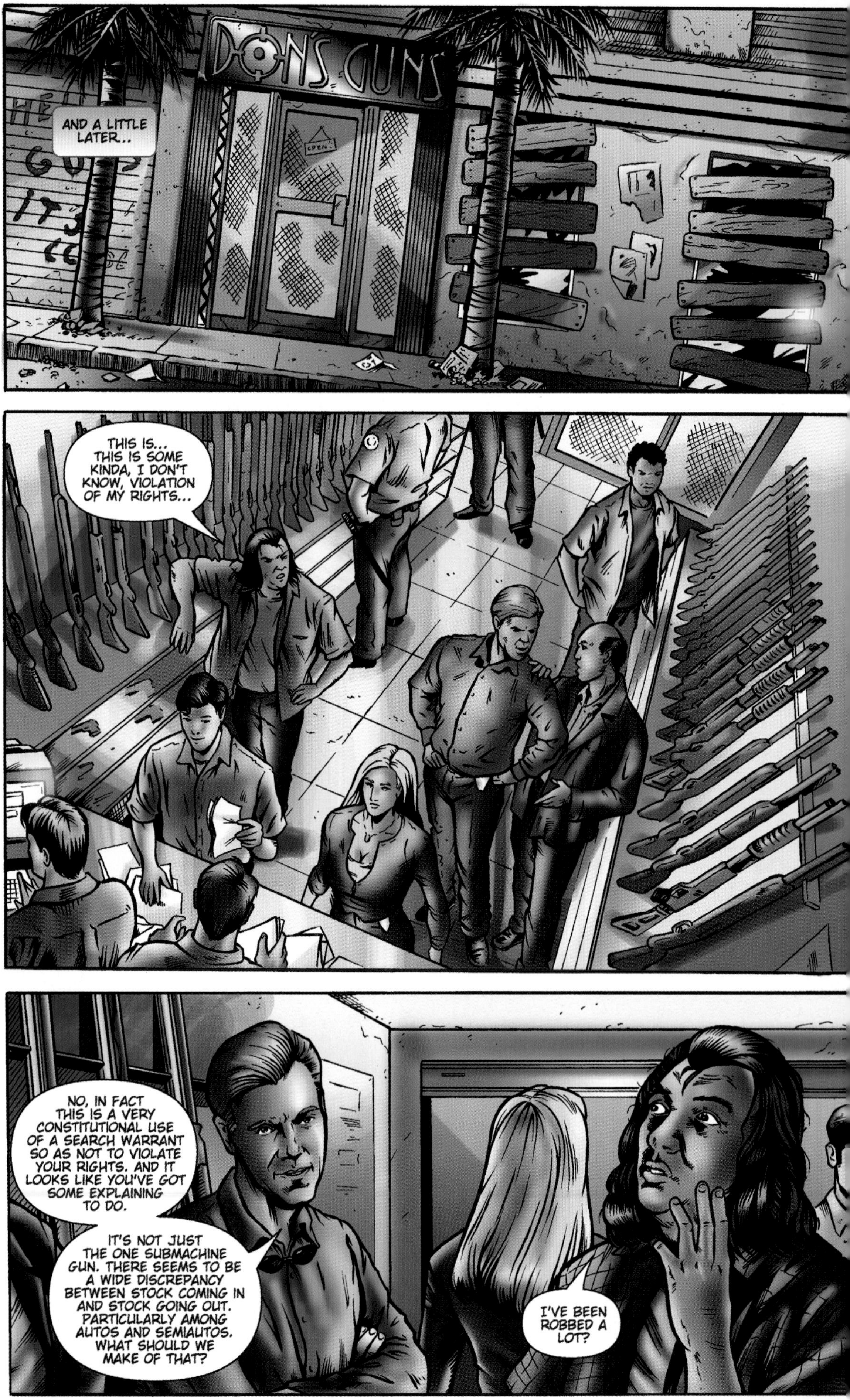
DON'S GUNS
AND A LITTLE LATER...
THIS IS... THIS IS SOME KINDA, I DON'T KNOW, VIOLATION OF MY RIGHTS...
NO, IN FACT THIS IS A VERY CONSTITUTIONAL USE OF A SEARCH WARRANT SO AS NOT TO VIOLATE YOUR RIGHTS. AND IT LOOKS LIKE YOU'VE GOT SOME EXPLAINING TO DO.
IT'S NOT JUST THE ONE SUBMACHINE GUN. THERE SEEMS TO BE A WIDE DISCREPANCY BETWEEN STOCK COMING IN AND STOCK GOING OUT. PARTICULARLY AMONG AUTOS AND SEMIAUTOS. WHAT SHOULD WE MAKE OF THAT?
I'VE BEEN ROBBED A LOT?

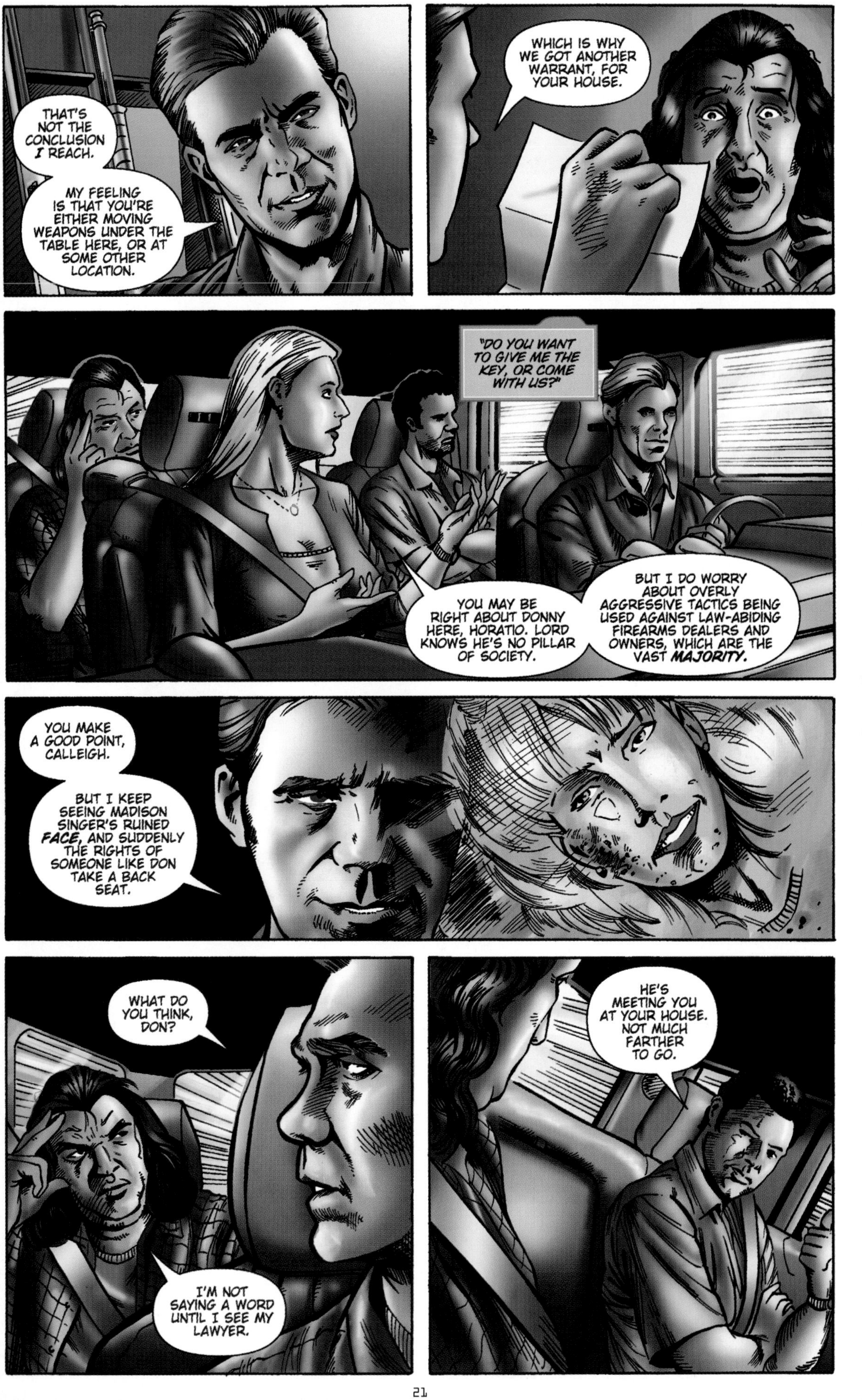
THAT'S NOT THE CONCLUSION I REACH.
MY FEELING IS THAT YOU'RE EITHER MOVING WEAPONS UNDER THE TABLE HERE, OR AT SOME OTHER LOCATION.
WHICH IS WHY WE GOT ANOTHER WARRANT, FOR YOUR HOUSE.
"DO YOU WANT TO GIVE ME THE KEY, OR COME WITH US?"
YOU MAY BE RIGHT ABOUT DONNY HERE, HORATIO. LORD KNOWS HE'S NO PILLAR OF SOCIETY.
BUT I DO WORRY ABOUT OVERLY AGGRESSIVE TACTICS BEING USED AGAINST LAW-ABIDING FIREARMS DEALERS AND OWNERS, WHICH ARE THE VAST MAJORITY.
YOU MAKE A GOOD POINT, CALLEIGH.
BUT I KEEP SEEING MADISON SINGER'S RUINED FACE, AND SUDDENLY THE RIGHTS OF SOMEONE LIKE DON TAKE A BACK SEAT.
WHAT DO YOU THINK, DON?
I'M NOT SAYING A WORD UNTIL I SEE MY LAWYER.
HE'S MEETING YOU AT YOUR HOUSE. NOT MUCH FARTHER TO GO.

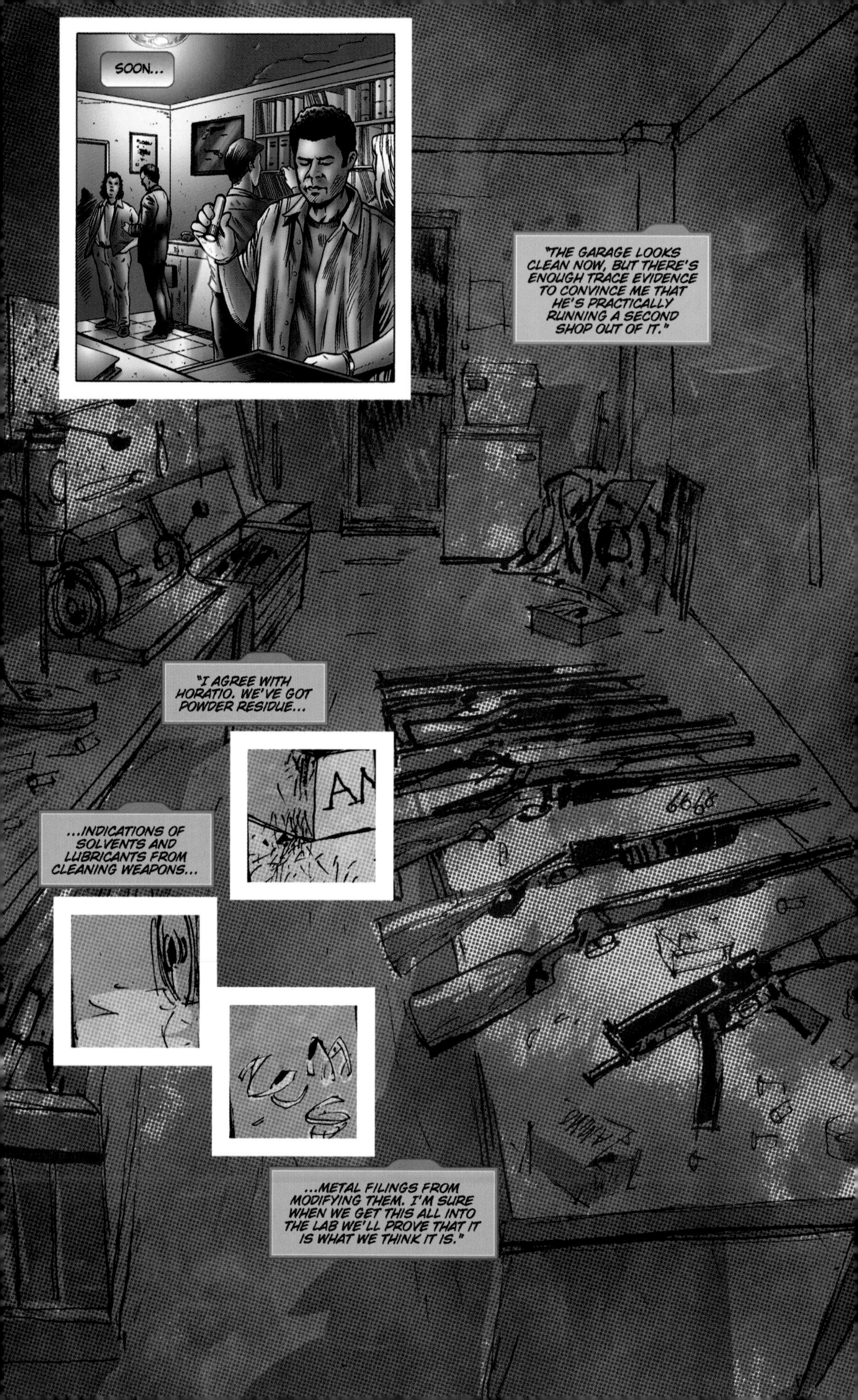
SOON...
"THE GARAGE LOOKS CLEAN NOW, BUT THERE'S ENOUGH TRACE EVIDENCE TO CONVINCE ME THAT HE'S PRACTICALLY RUNNING A SECOND SHOP OUT OF IT."
"I AGREE WITH HORATIO. WE'VE GOT POWDER RESIDUE...
...INDICATIONS OF SOLVENTS AND LUBRICANTS FROM CLEANING WEAPONS...
...METAL FILINGS FROM MODIFYING THEM. I'M SURE WHEN WE GET THIS ALL INTO THE LAB WE'LL PROVE THAT IT IS WHAT WE THINK IT IS."

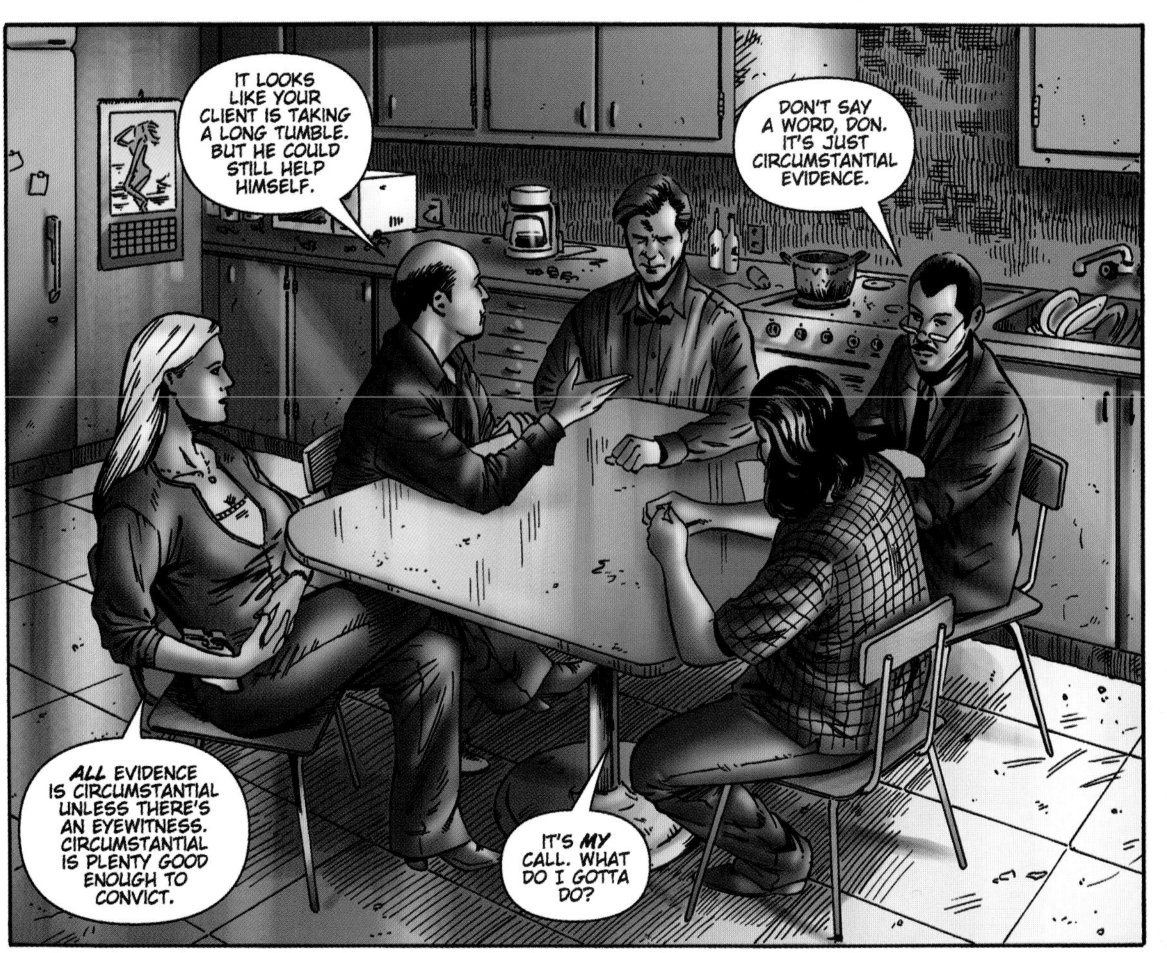
IT LOOKS LIKE YOUR CLIENT IS TAKING A LONG TUMBLE. BUT HE COULD STILL HELP HIMSELF.
DON'T SAY A WORD, DON. IT'S JUST CIRCUMSTANTIAL EVIDENCE.
ALL EVIDENCE IS CIRCUMSTANTIAL UNLESS THERE'S AN EYEWITNESS. CIRCUMSTANTIAL IS PLENTY GOOD ENOUGH TO CONVICT.
IT'S MY CALL. WHAT DO I GOTTA DO?

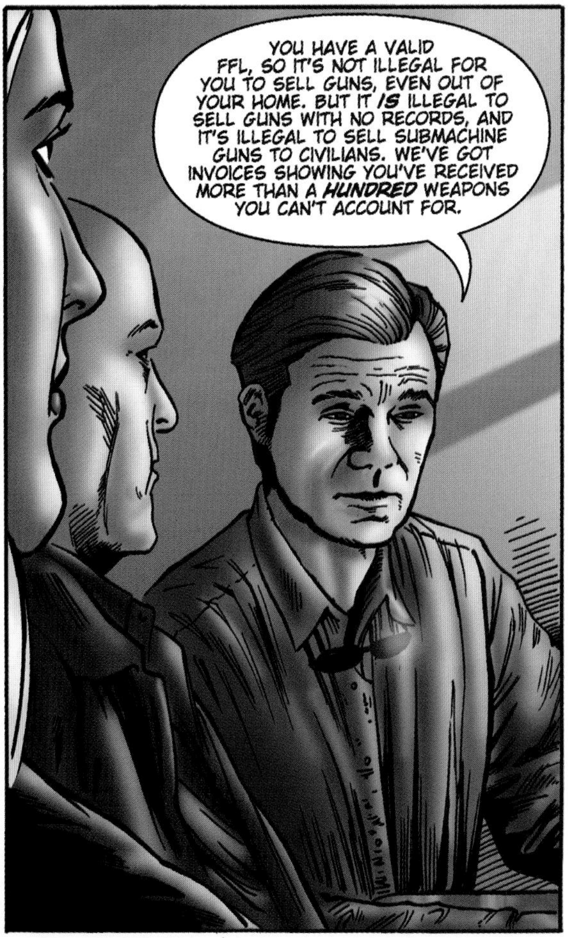
YOU HAVE A VALID FFL, SO IT'S NOT ILLEGAL FOR YOU TO SELL GUNS, EVEN OUT OF YOUR HOME. BUT IT IS ILLEGAL TO SELL GUNS WITH NO RECORDS, AND IT'S ILLEGAL TO SELL SUBMACHINE GUNS TO CIVILIANS. WE'VE GOT INVOICES SHOWING YOU'VE RECEIVED MORE THAN A HUNDRED WEAPONS YOU CAN'T ACCOUNT FOR.

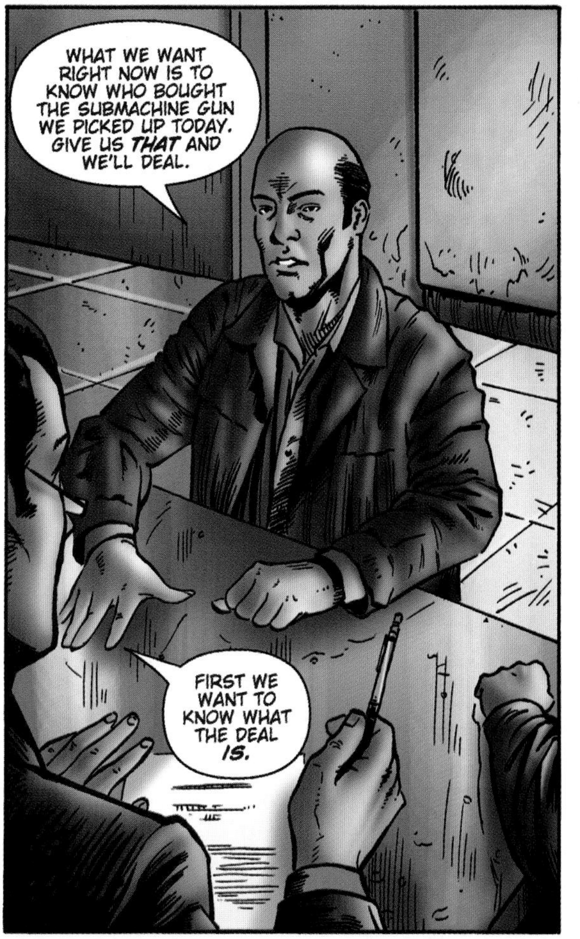
WHAT WE WANT RIGHT NOW IS TO KNOW WHO BOUGHT THE SUBMACHINE GUN WE PICKED UP TODAY. GIVE US THAT AND WE'LL DEAL.
FIRST WE WANT TO KNOW WHAT THE DEAL IS.

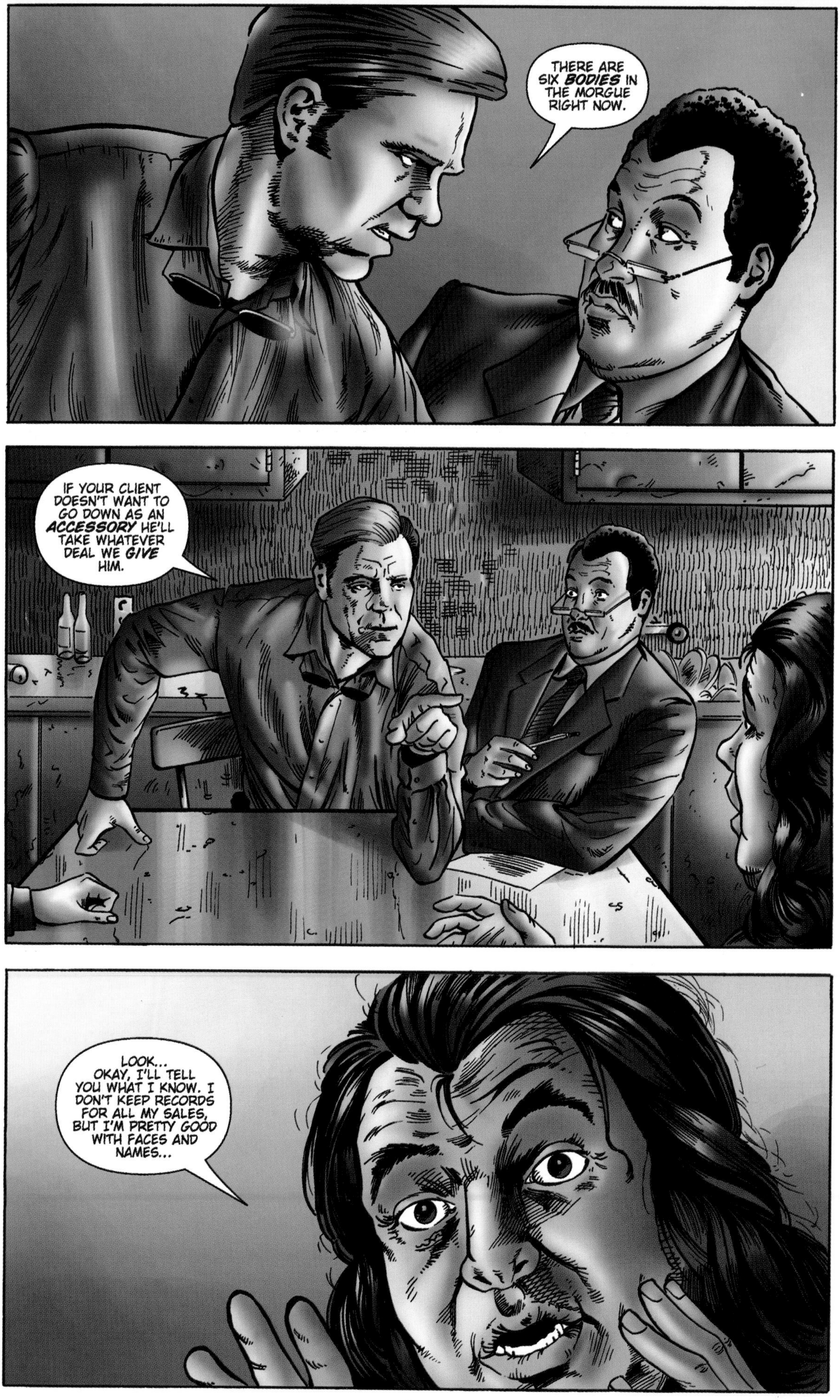
THERE ARE SIX BODIES IN THE MORGUE RIGHT NOW.
IF YOUR CLIENT DOESN'T WANT TO GO DOWN AS AN ACCESSORY HE'LL TAKE WHATEVER DEAL WE GIVE HIM.
LOOK... OKAY, I'LL TELL YOU WHAT I KNOW. I DON'T KEEP RECORDS FOR ALL MY SALES, BUT I'M PRETTY GOOD WITH FACES AND NAMES...

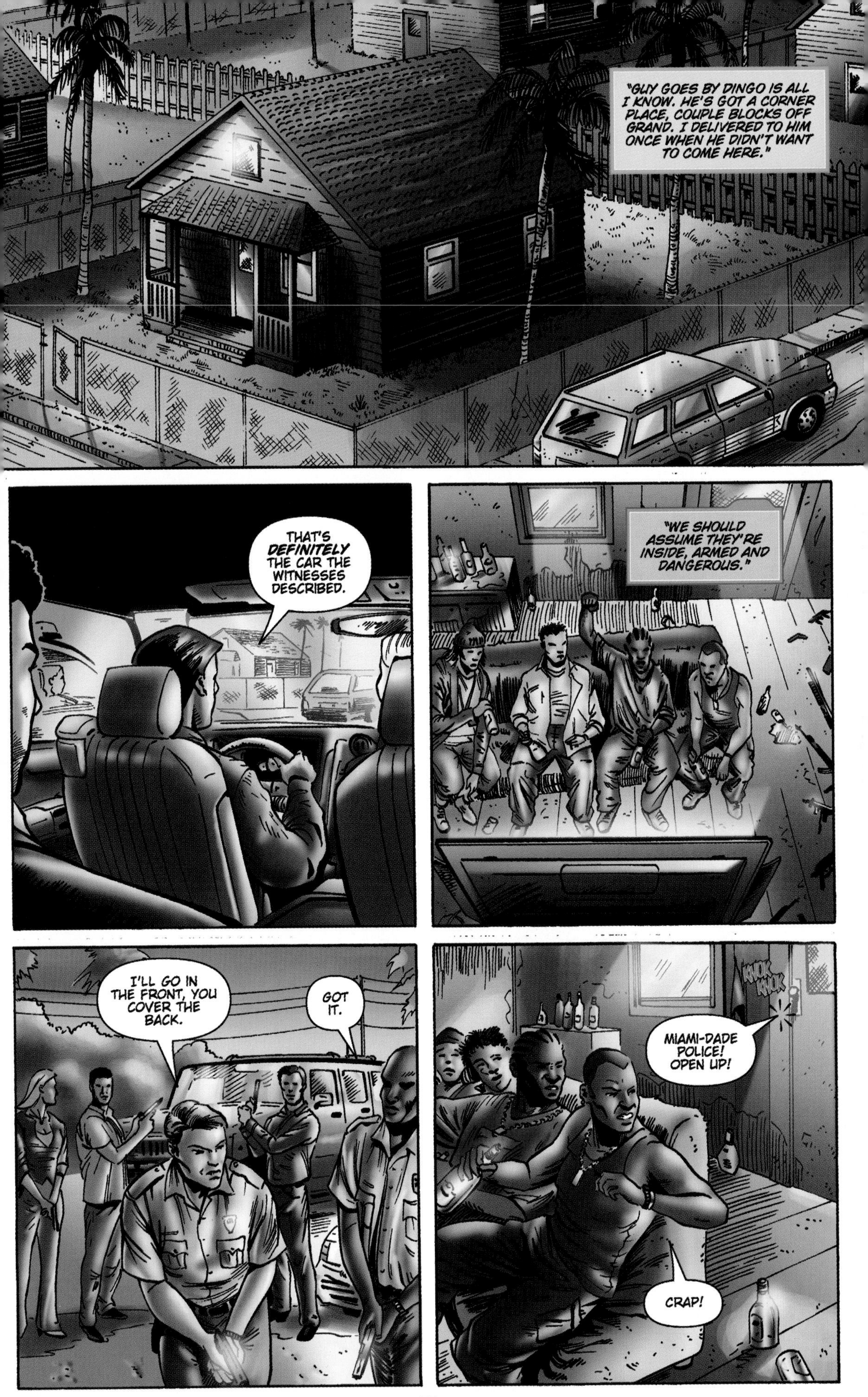
"GUY GOES BY DINGO IS ALL I KNOW. HE'S GOT A CORNER PLACE, COUPLE BLOCKS OFF GRAND. I DELIVERED TO HIM ONCE WHEN HE DIDN'T WANT TO COME HERE."
THAT'S *DEFINITELY* THE CAR THE WITNESSES DESCRIBED.
"WE SHOULD ASSUME THEY'RE INSIDE, ARMED AND DANGEROUS."
I'LL GO IN THE FRONT, YOU COVER THE BACK.
GOT IT.
KNOK KNOK
MIAMI-DADE POLICE! OPEN UP!
CRAP!

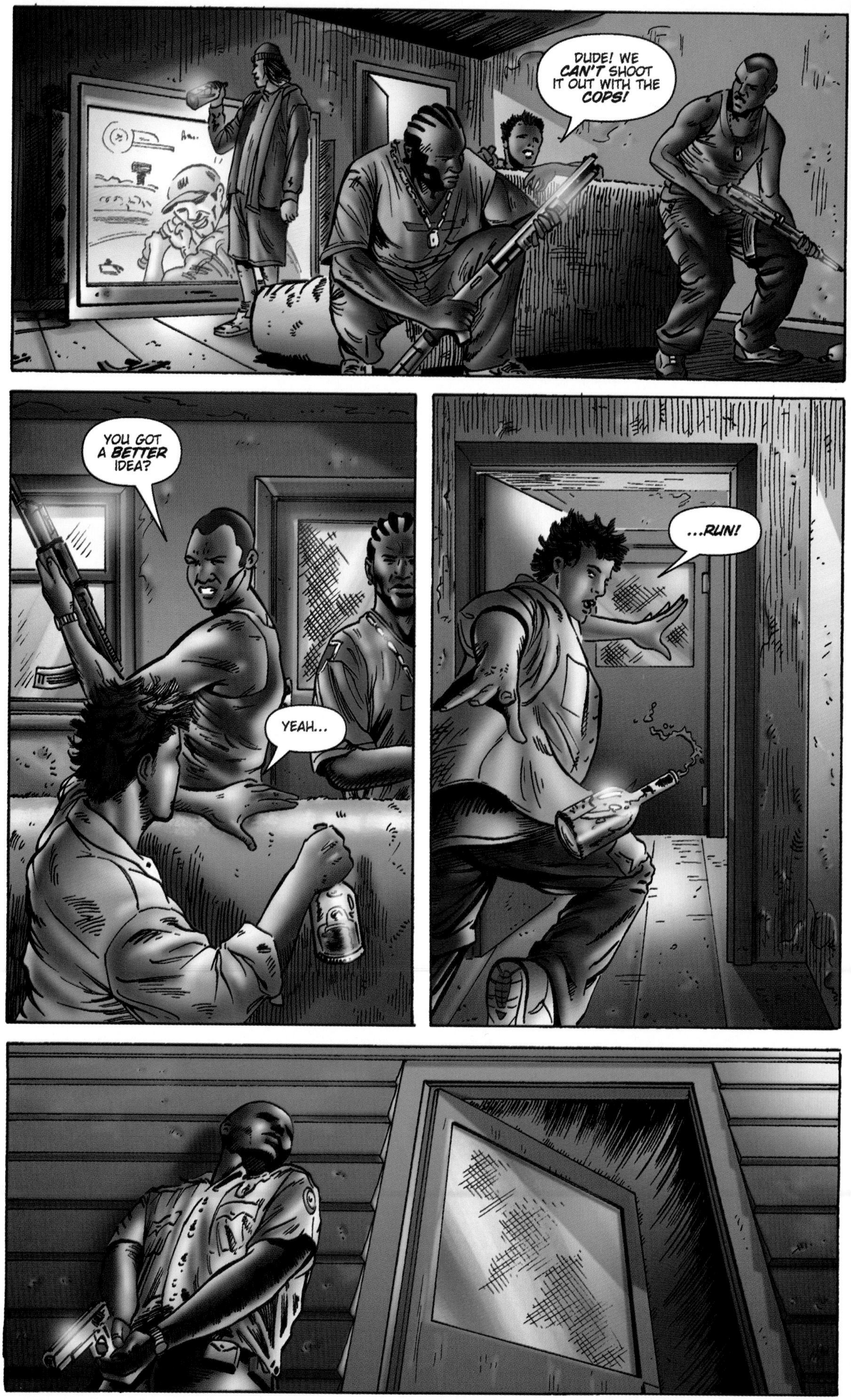
DUDE! WE CAN'T SHOOT IT OUT WITH THE COPS!
YOU GOT A BETTER IDEA?
YEAH...
...RUN!

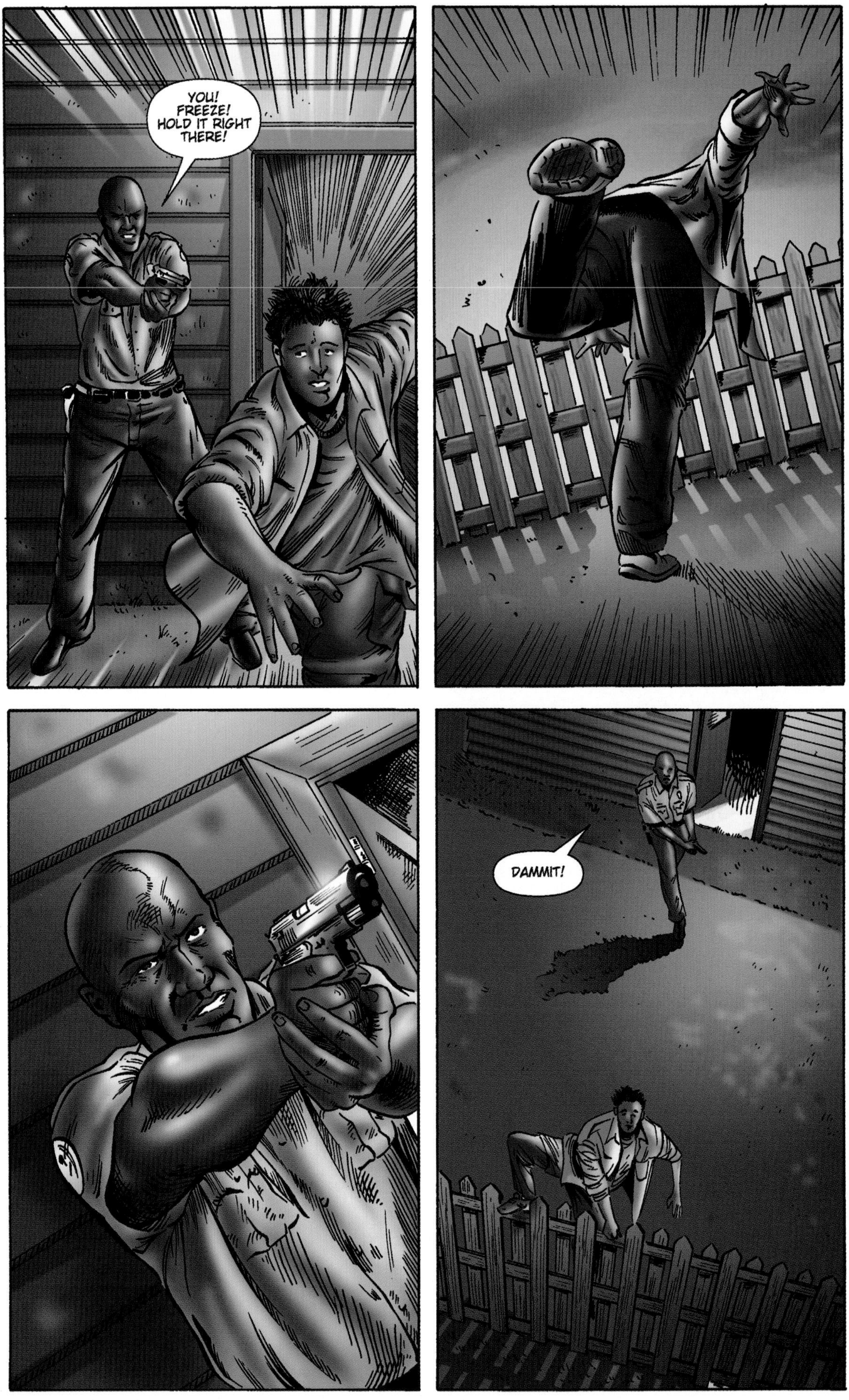
YOU! FREEZE! HOLD IT RIGHT THERE!
DAMMIT!

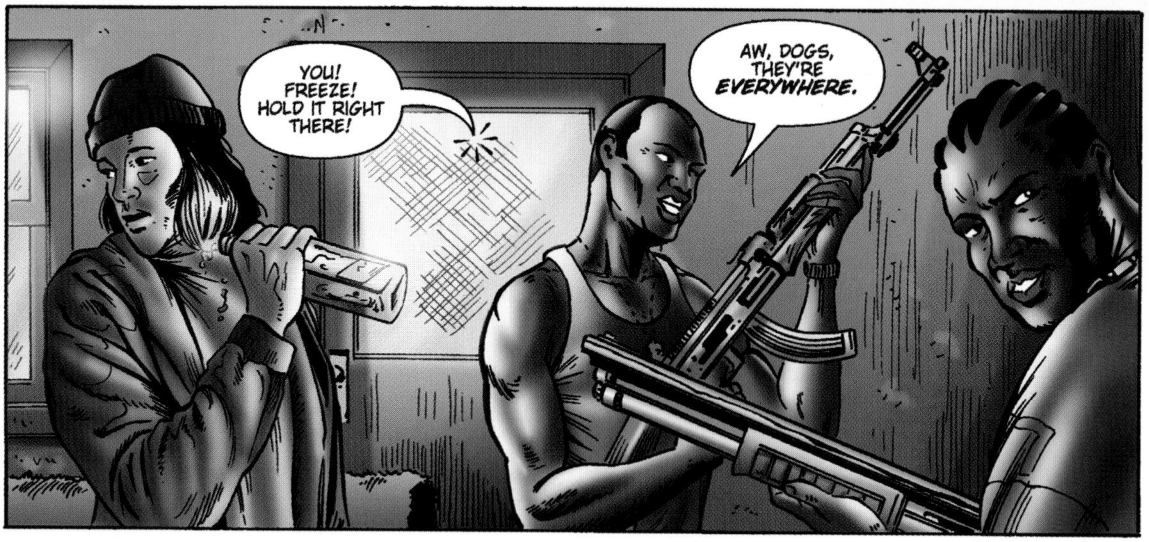
YOU! FREEZE! HOLD IT RIGHT THERE!
AW, DOGS, THEY'RE *EVERYWHERE.*

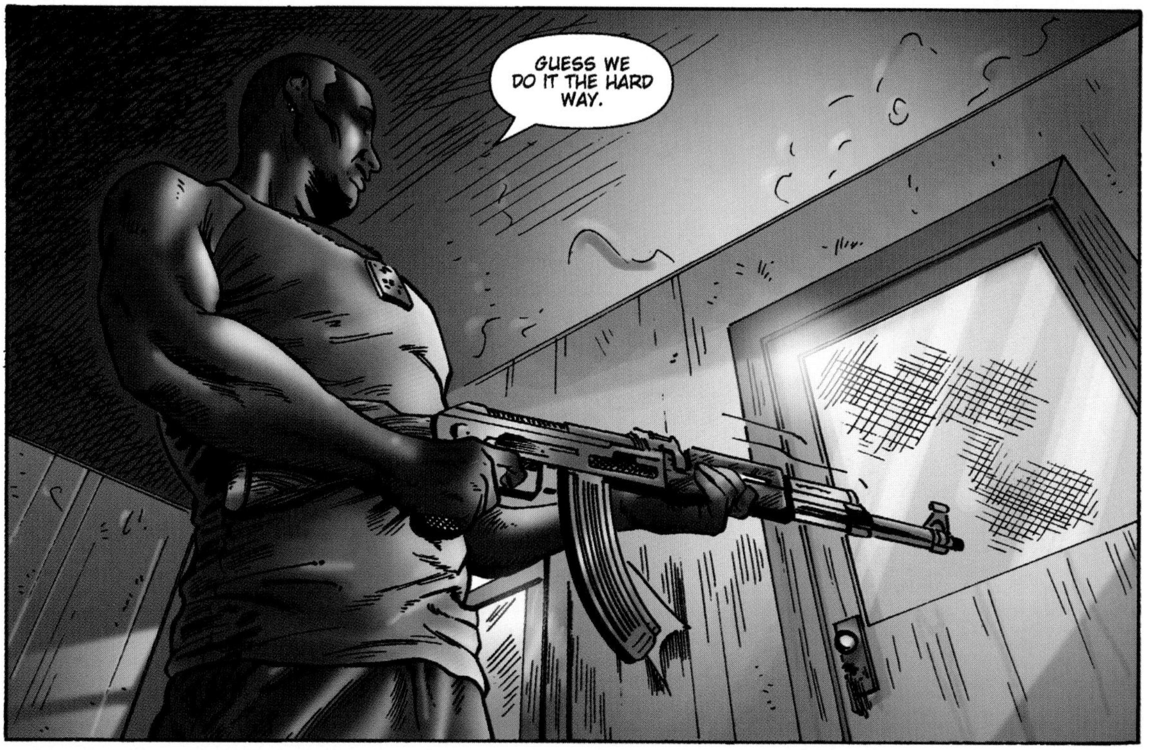
GUESS WE DO IT THE HARD WAY.

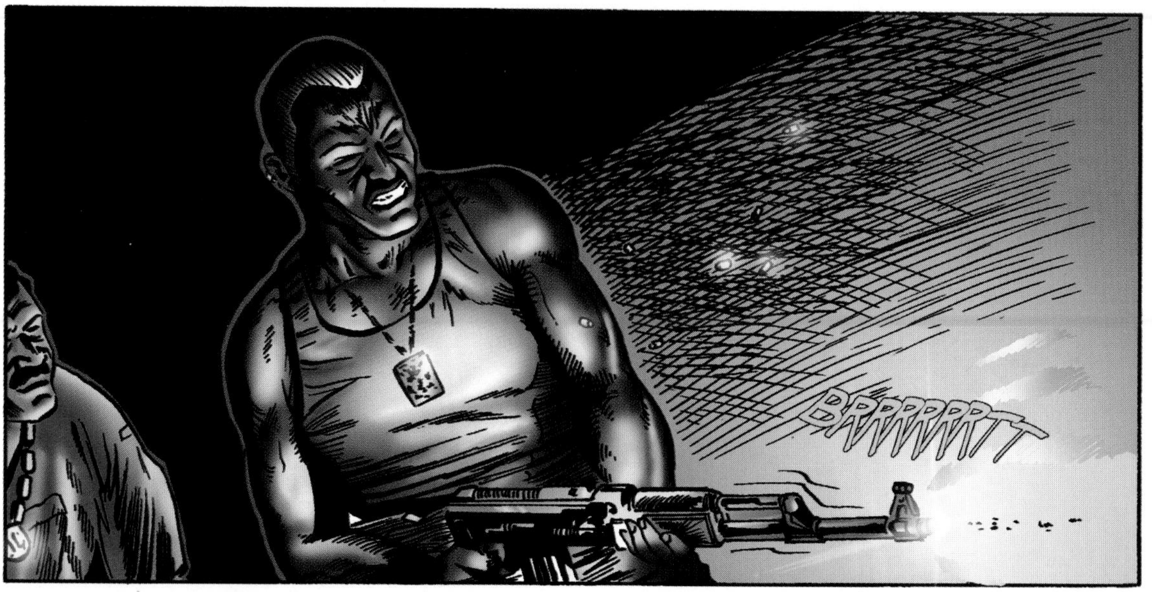
BRRRRRRRTT

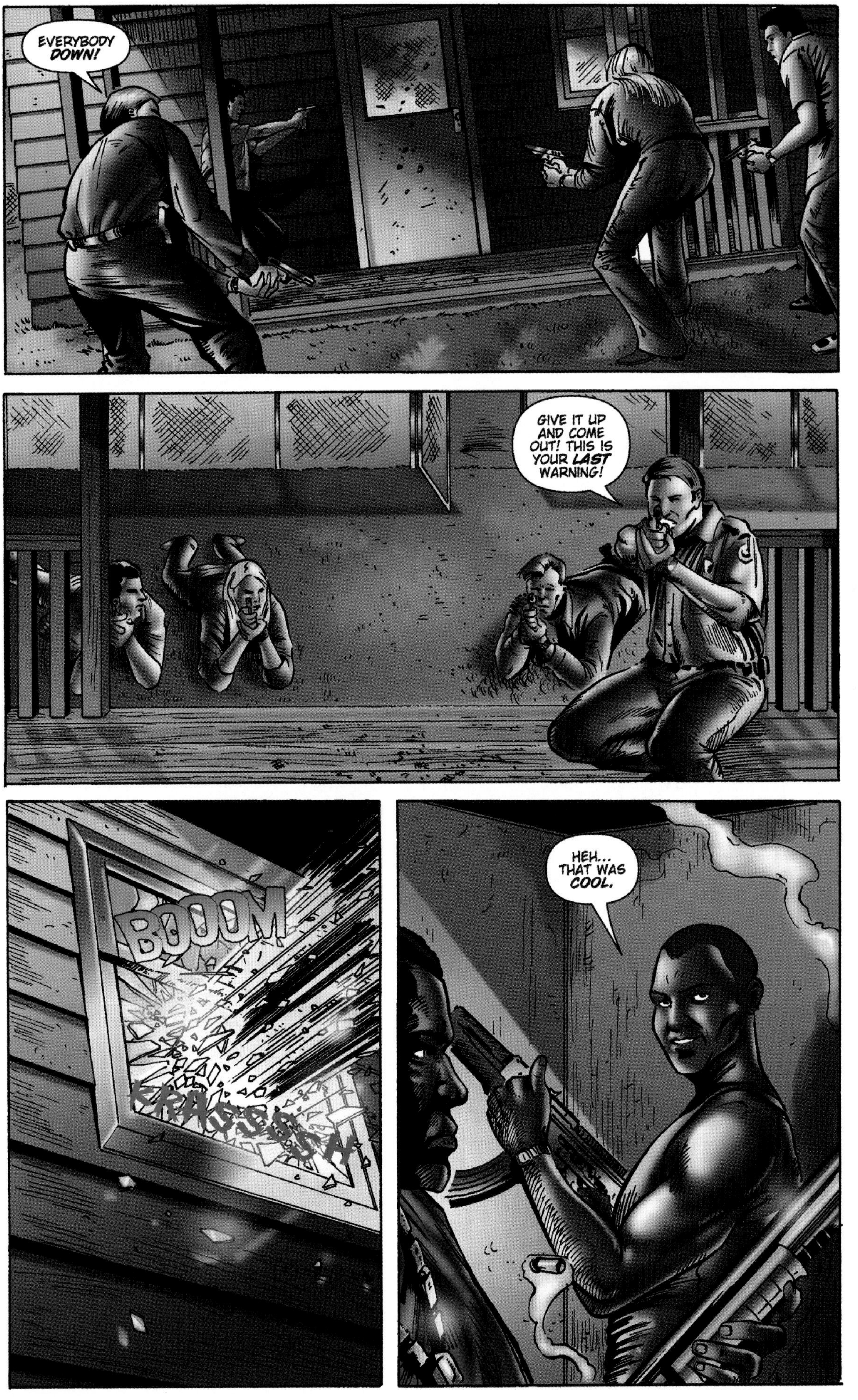
EVERYBODY DOWN!
GIVE IT UP AND COME OUT! THIS IS YOUR LAST WARNING!
BOOOM
KRASSSSH
HEH... THAT WAS COOL.

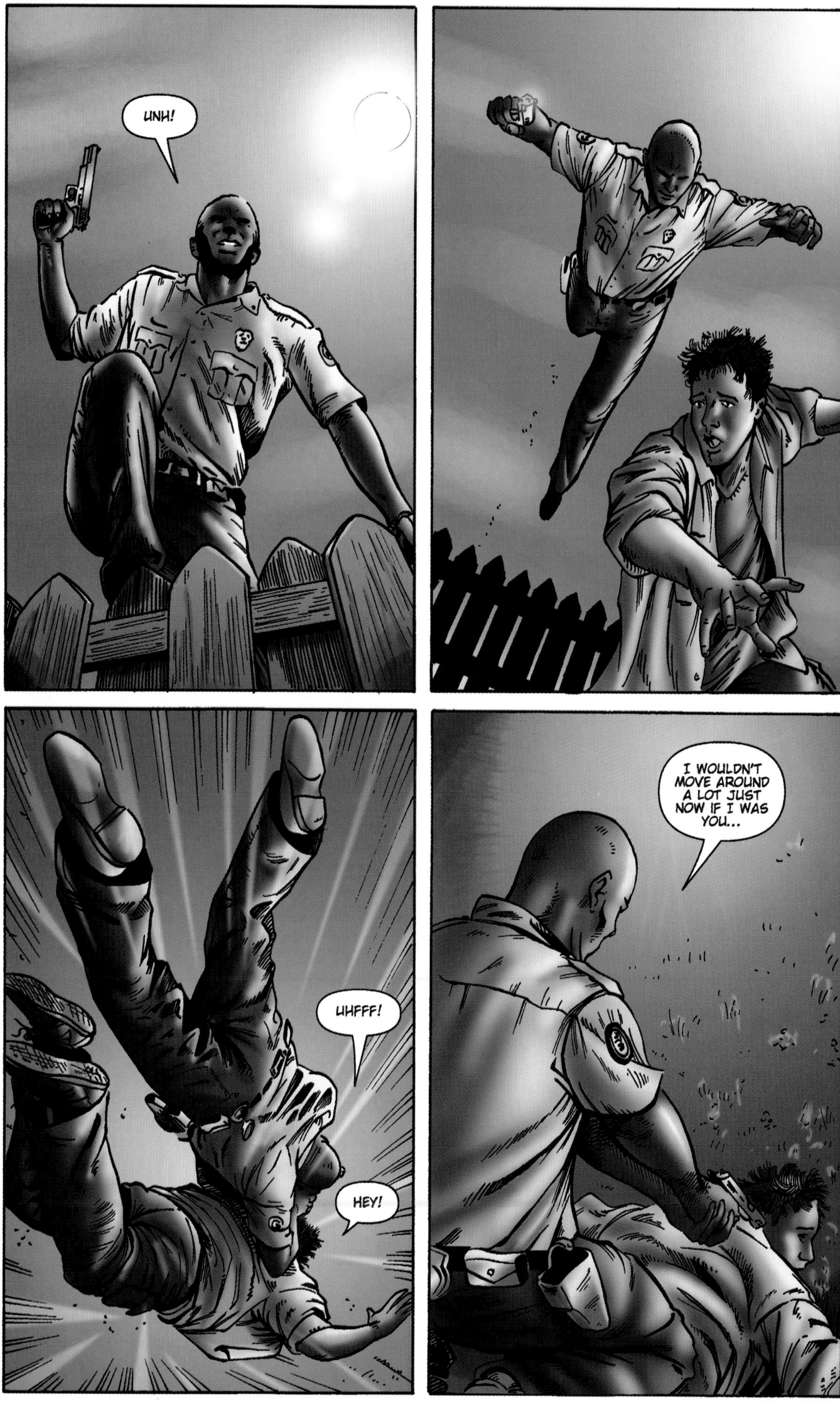
UNH!
UHFFF!
HEY!
I WOULDN'T MOVE AROUND A LOT JUST NOW IF I WAS YOU...

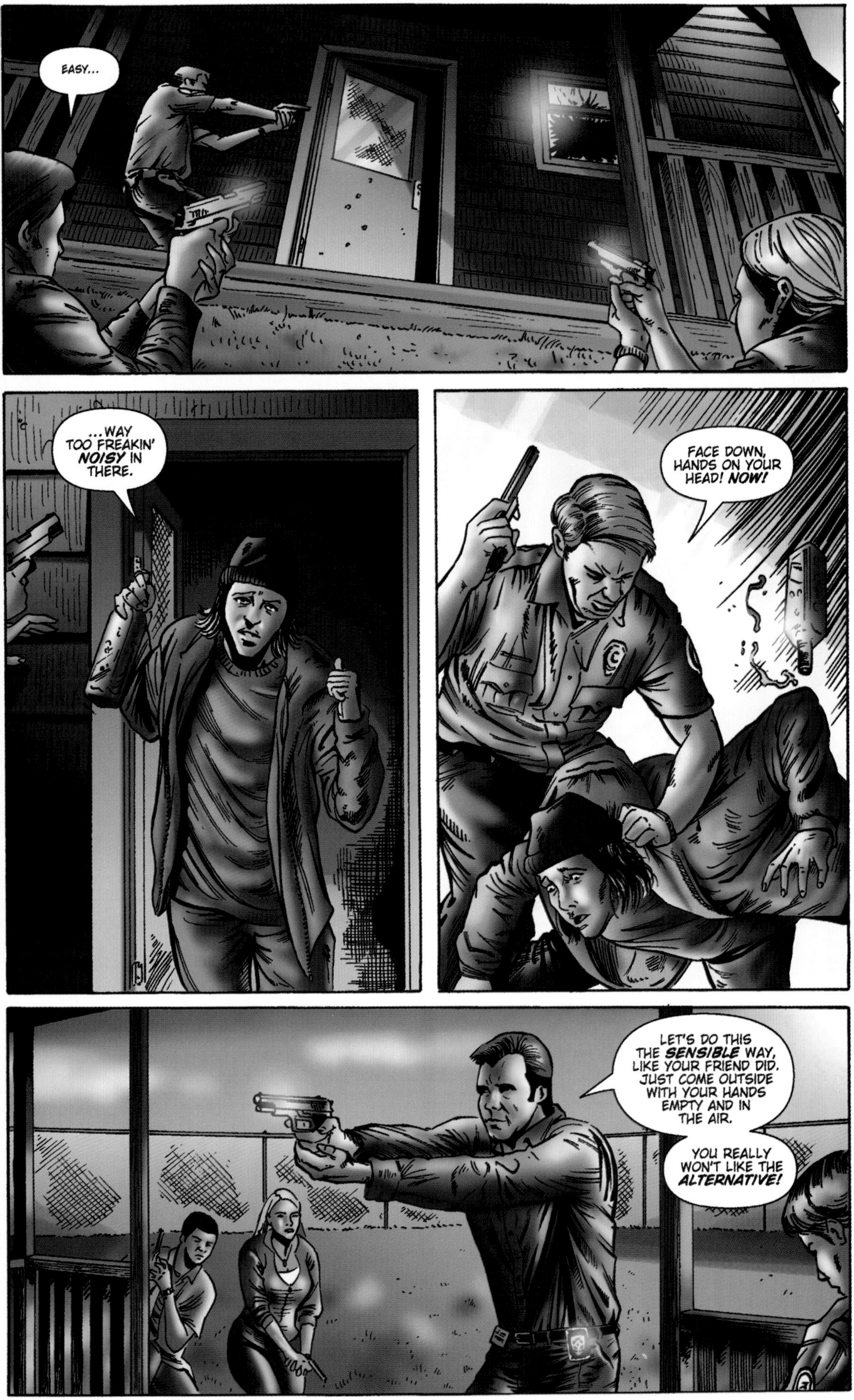
EASY...
...WAY TOO FREAKIN' NOISY IN THERE.
FACE DOWN, HANDS ON YOUR HEAD! NOW!
LET'S DO THIS THE SENSIBLE WAY, LIKE YOUR FRIEND DID. JUST COME OUTSIDE WITH YOUR HANDS EMPTY AND IN THE AIR.
YOU REALLY WON'T LIKE THE ALTERNATIVE!

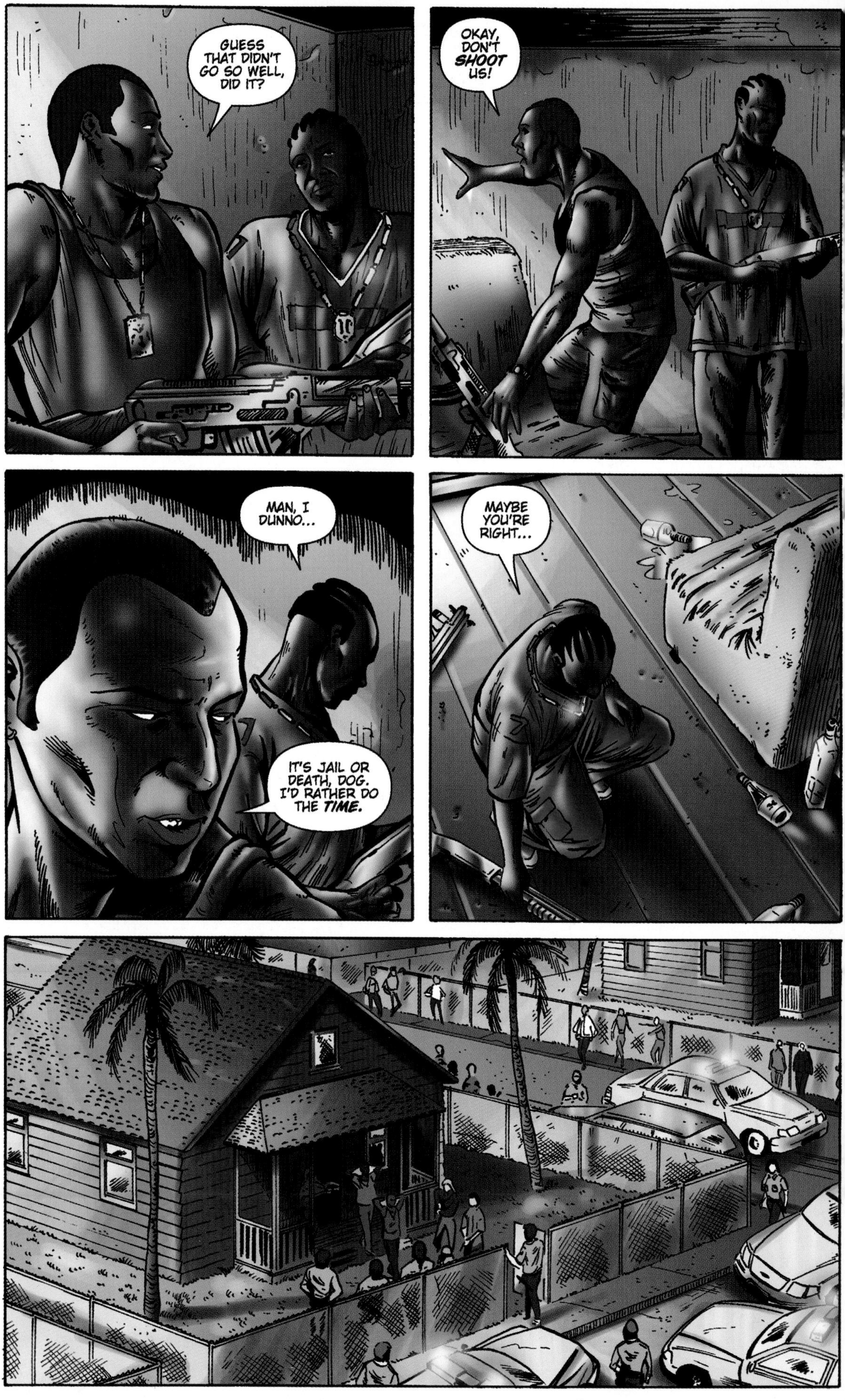
GUESS THAT DIDN'T GO SO WELL, DID IT?
OKAY, DON'T SHOOT US!
MAN, I DUNNO...
IT'S JAIL OR DEATH, DOG. I'D RATHER DO THE TIME.
MAYBE YOU'RE RIGHT...

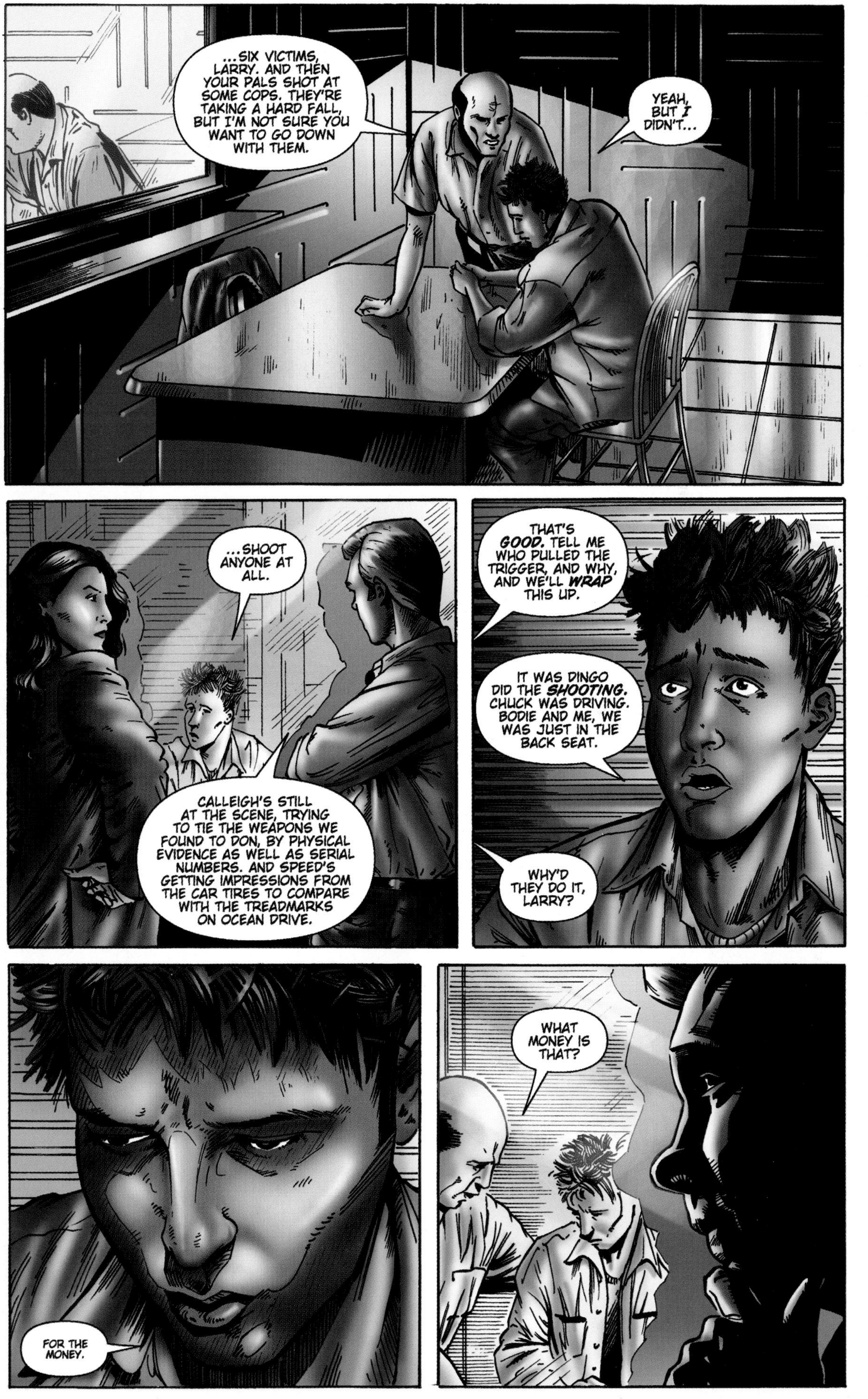
...SIX VICTIMS, LARRY. AND THEN YOUR PALS SHOT AT SOME COPS. THEY'RE TAKING A HARD FALL, BUT I'M NOT SURE YOU WANT TO GO DOWN WITH THEM.
YEAH, BUT *I* DIDN'T...
...SHOOT ANYONE AT ALL.
CALLEIGH'S STILL AT THE SCENE, TRYING TO TIE THE WEAPONS WE FOUND TO DON, BY PHYSICAL EVIDENCE AS WELL AS SERIAL NUMBERS. AND SPEED'S GETTING IMPRESSIONS FROM THE CAR TIRES TO COMPARE WITH THE TREADMARKS ON OCEAN DRIVE.
THAT'S ***GOOD.*** TELL ME WHO PULLED THE TRIGGER, AND WHY, AND WE'LL ***WRAP*** THIS UP.
IT WAS DINGO DID THE ***SHOOTING.*** CHUCK WAS DRIVING. BODIE AND ME, WE WAS JUST IN THE BACK SEAT.
WHY'D THEY DO IT, LARRY?
FOR THE MONEY.
WHAT MONEY IS THAT?

THIS SHOULD BE GOOD.

WE GOT *PAID* TO SHOOT UP THE BLOCK. HALF UP FRONT, HALF AFTER. STILL HAVEN'T SEEN *THAT* HALF YET.

YOU KILLED PEOPLE FOR MONEY AND YOU EXPECT THE PERSON WHO HIRED YOU TO BE *HONEST?* YOU *ARE* DUMBER THAN YOU LOOK.

WE DIDN'T *MEAN* TO KILL ANYONE. WE WAS JUST STIRRING UP SOME TROUBLE, Y'KNOW? *SCARING* PEOPLE.

WHO WAS IT?

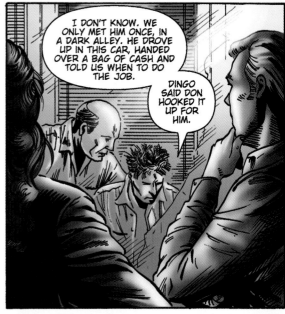

I DON'T KNOW. WE ONLY MET HIM ONCE, IN A DARK ALLEY. HE DROVE UP IN THIS CAR, HANDED OVER A BAG OF CASH AND TOLD US WHEN TO DO THE JOB.

DINGO SAID DON HOOKED IT UP FOR HIM.

DON FISCHER, THE *GUN SHOP* OWNER?

THAT'S RIGHT. DINGO'S BEEN A CUSTOMER OF HIS FOR YEARS.

IT LOOKS LIKE WHATEVER DEAL DON CUT JUST WENT OUT THE *WINDOW.*

34

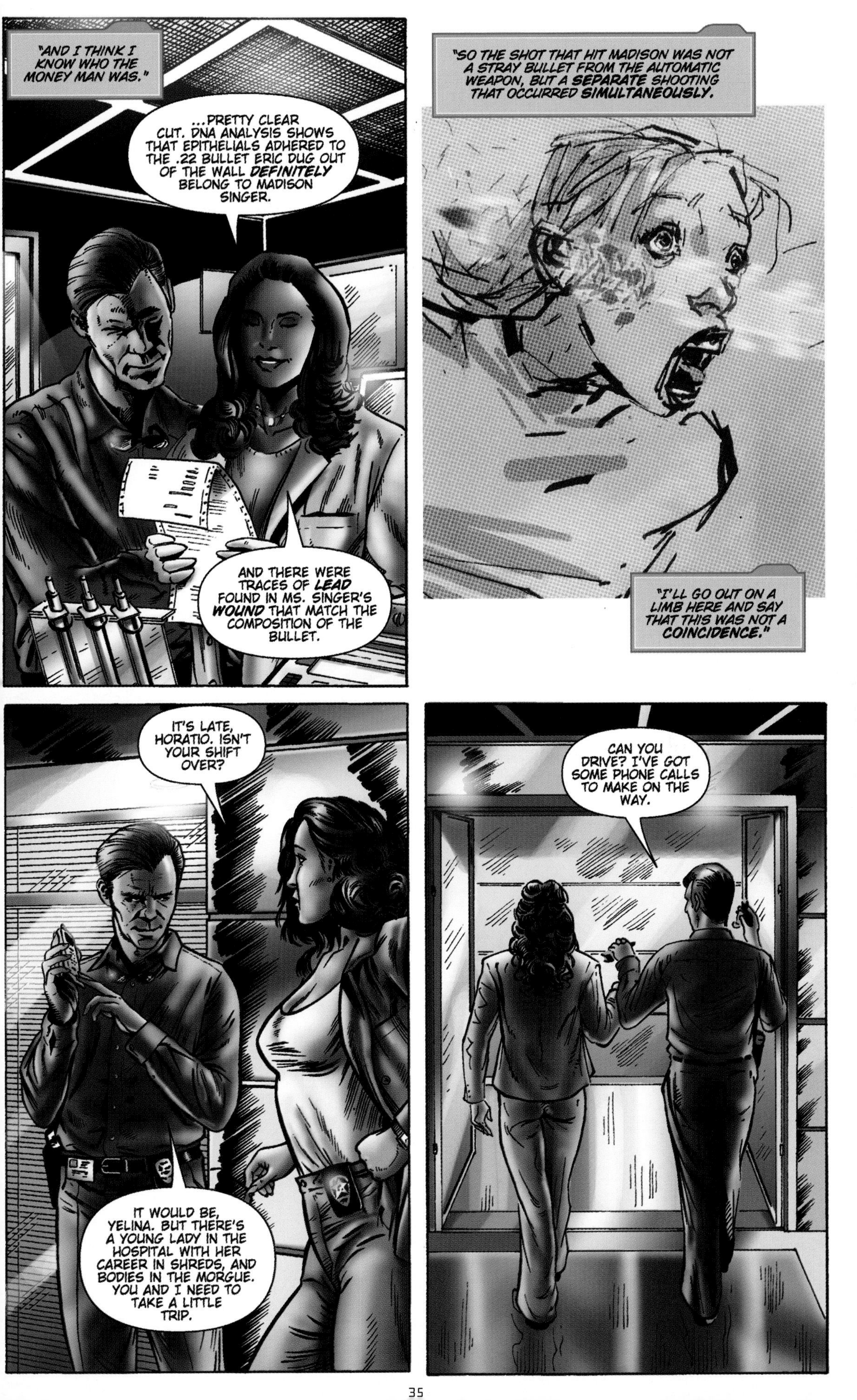
"AND I THINK I KNOW WHO THE MONEY MAN WAS."
...PRETTY CLEAR CUT. DNA ANALYSIS SHOWS THAT EPITHELIALS ADHERED TO THE .22 BULLET ERIC DUG OUT OF THE WALL DEFINITELY BELONG TO MADISON SINGER.
AND THERE WERE TRACES OF LEAD FOUND IN MS. SINGER'S WOUND THAT MATCH THE COMPOSITION OF THE BULLET.
"SO THE SHOT THAT HIT MADISON WAS NOT A STRAY BULLET FROM THE AUTOMATIC WEAPON, BUT A SEPARATE SHOOTING THAT OCCURRED SIMULTANEOUSLY.
"I'LL GO OUT ON A LIMB HERE AND SAY THAT THIS WAS NOT A COINCIDENCE."
IT'S LATE, HORATIO. ISN'T YOUR SHIFT OVER?
IT WOULD BE, YELINA. BUT THERE'S A YOUNG LADY IN THE HOSPITAL WITH HER CAREER IN SHREDS, AND BODIES IN THE MORGUE. YOU AND I NEED TO TAKE A LITTLE TRIP.
CAN YOU DRIVE? I'VE GOT SOME PHONE CALLS TO MAKE ON THE WAY.

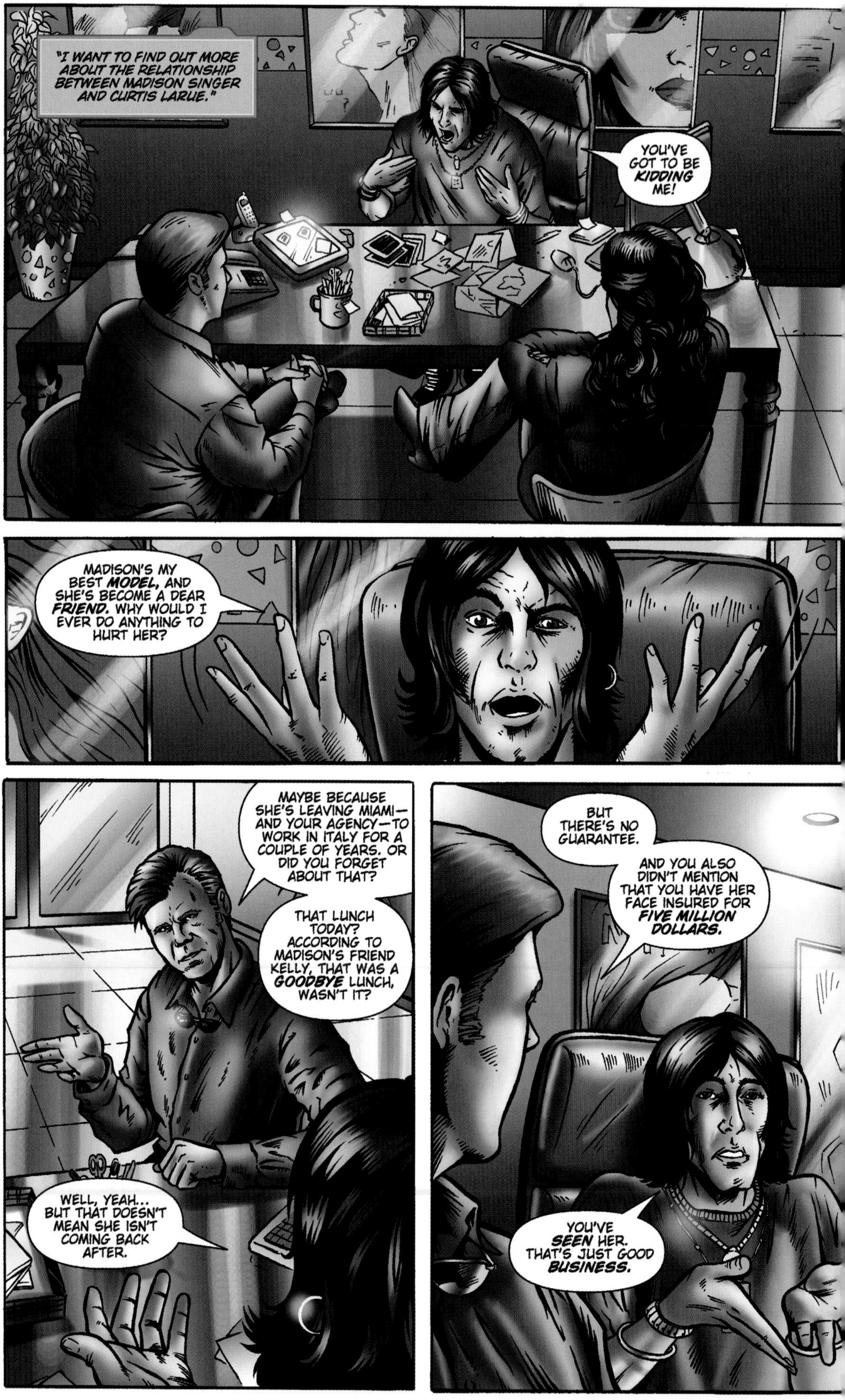
"I WANT TO FIND OUT MORE ABOUT THE RELATIONSHIP BETWEEN MADISON SINGER AND CURTIS LARUE."
YOU'VE GOT TO BE KIDDING ME!
MADISON'S MY BEST MODEL, AND SHE'S BECOME A DEAR FRIEND. WHY WOULD I EVER DO ANYTHING TO HURT HER?
MAYBE BECAUSE SHE'S LEAVING MIAMI— AND YOUR AGENCY—TO WORK IN ITALY FOR A COUPLE OF YEARS. OR DID YOU FORGET ABOUT THAT?
THAT LUNCH TODAY? ACCORDING TO MADISON'S FRIEND KELLY, THAT WAS A GOODBYE LUNCH, WASN'T IT?
WELL, YEAH... BUT THAT DOESN'T MEAN SHE ISN'T COMING BACK AFTER.
BUT THERE'S NO GUARANTEE.
AND YOU ALSO DIDN'T MENTION THAT YOU HAVE HER FACE INSURED FOR FIVE MILLION DOLLARS.
YOU'VE SEEN HER. THAT'S JUST GOOD BUSINESS.

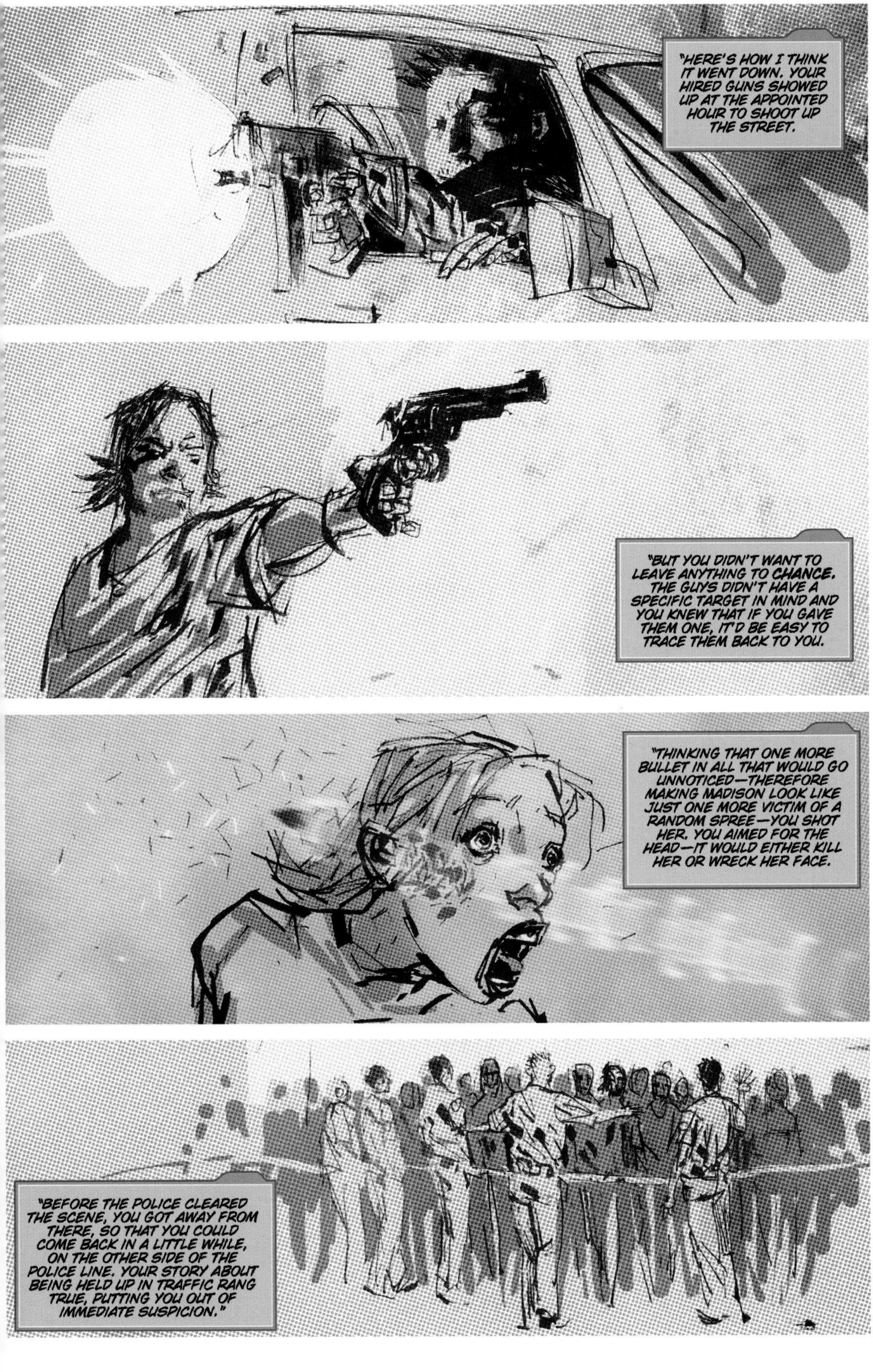
"HERE'S HOW I THINK IT WENT DOWN. YOUR HIRED GUNS SHOWED UP AT THE APPOINTED HOUR TO SHOOT UP THE STREET.
"BUT YOU DIDN'T WANT TO LEAVE ANYTHING TO CHANCE. THE GUYS DIDN'T HAVE A SPECIFIC TARGET IN MIND AND YOU KNEW THAT IF YOU GAVE THEM ONE, IT'D BE EASY TO TRACE THEM BACK TO YOU.
"THINKING THAT ONE MORE BULLET IN ALL THAT WOULD GO UNNOTICED—THEREFORE MAKING MADISON LOOK LIKE JUST ONE MORE VICTIM OF A RANDOM SPREE—YOU SHOT HER. YOU AIMED FOR THE HEAD—IT WOULD EITHER KILL HER OR WRECK HER FACE.
"BEFORE THE POLICE CLEARED THE SCENE, YOU GOT AWAY FROM THERE, SO THAT YOU COULD COME BACK IN A LITTLE WHILE, ON THE OTHER SIDE OF THE POLICE LINE. YOUR STORY ABOUT BEING HELD UP IN TRAFFIC RANG TRUE, PUTTING YOU OUT OF IMMEDIATE SUSPICION."

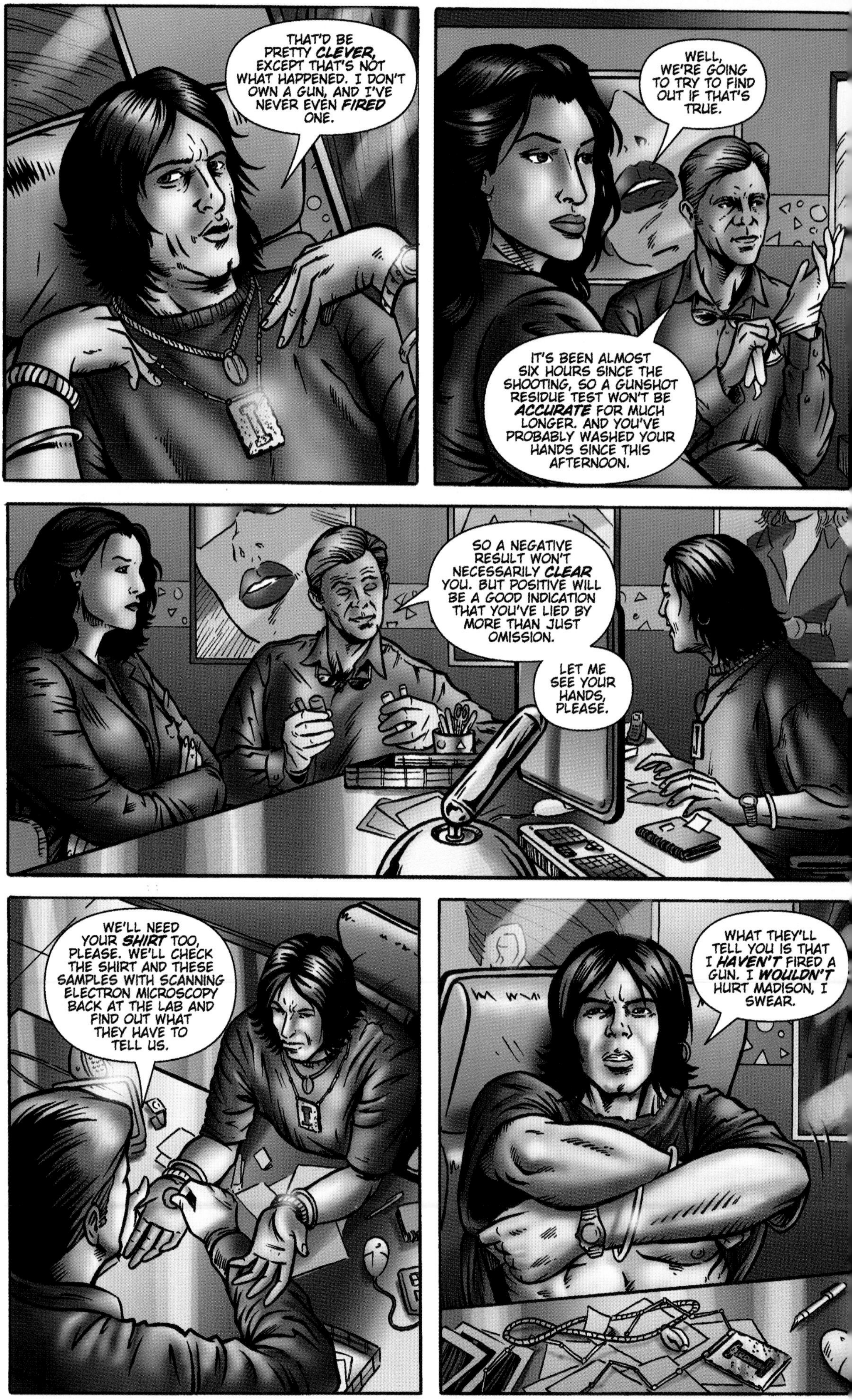
THAT'D BE PRETTY CLEVER, EXCEPT THAT'S NOT WHAT HAPPENED. I DON'T OWN A GUN, AND I'VE NEVER EVEN FIRED ONE.
WELL, WE'RE GOING TO TRY TO FIND OUT IF THAT'S TRUE.
IT'S BEEN ALMOST SIX HOURS SINCE THE SHOOTING, SO A GUNSHOT RESIDUE TEST WON'T BE ACCURATE FOR MUCH LONGER. AND YOU'VE PROBABLY WASHED YOUR HANDS SINCE THIS AFTERNOON.
SO A NEGATIVE RESULT WON'T NECESSARILY CLEAR YOU. BUT POSITIVE WILL BE A GOOD INDICATION THAT YOU'VE LIED BY MORE THAN JUST OMISSION.
LET ME SEE YOUR HANDS, PLEASE.
WE'LL NEED YOUR SHIRT TOO, PLEASE. WE'LL CHECK THE SHIRT AND THESE SAMPLES WITH SCANNING ELECTRON MICROSCOPY BACK AT THE LAB AND FIND OUT WHAT THEY HAVE TO TELL US.
WHAT THEY'LL TELL YOU IS THAT I HAVEN'T FIRED A GUN. I WOULDN'T HURT MADISON, I SWEAR.

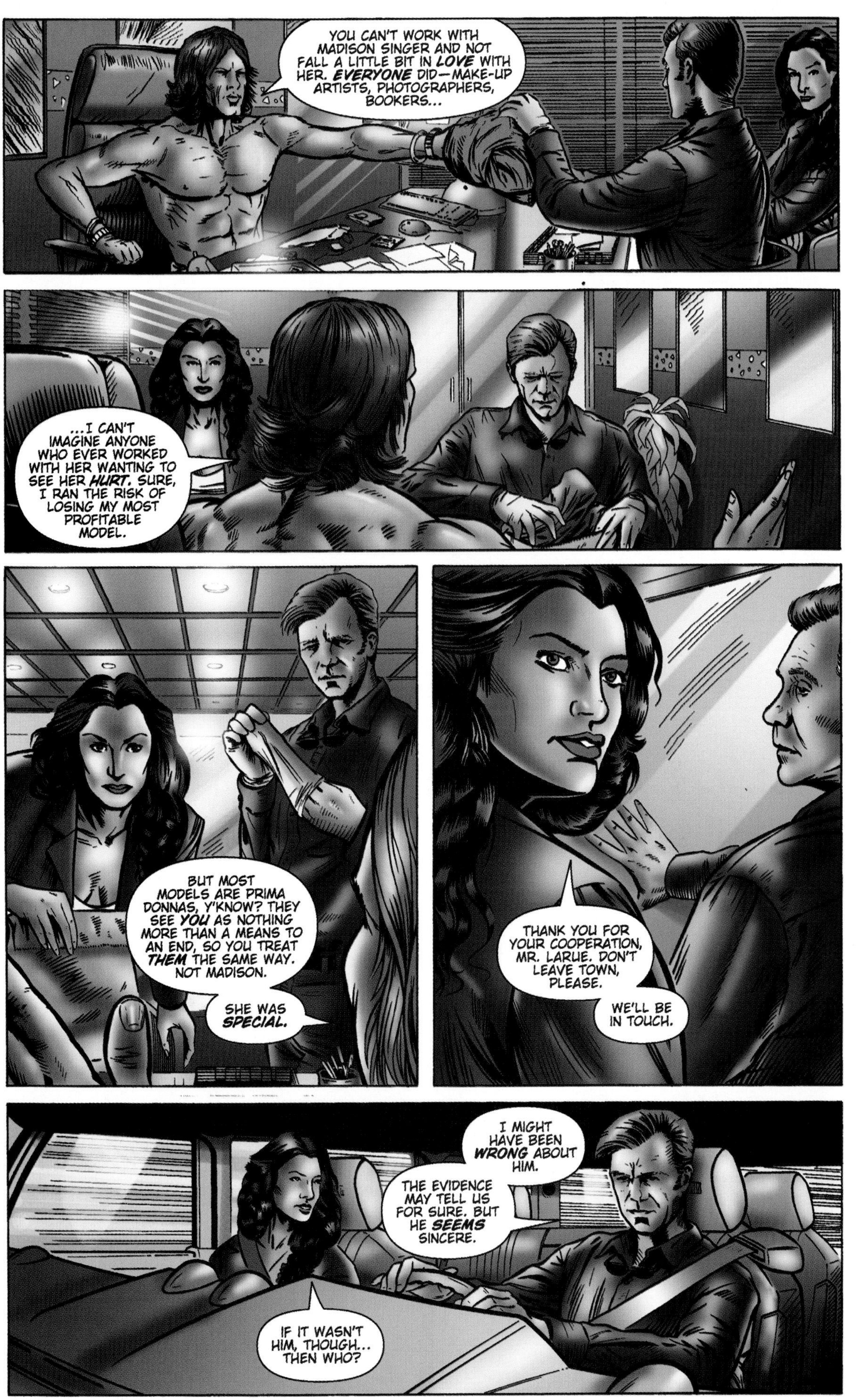
YOU CAN'T WORK WITH MADISON SINGER AND NOT FALL A LITTLE BIT IN LOVE WITH HER. EVERYONE DID—MAKE-UP ARTISTS, PHOTOGRAPHERS, BOOKERS...
...I CAN'T IMAGINE ANYONE WHO EVER WORKED WITH HER WANTING TO SEE HER HURT. SURE, I RAN THE RISK OF LOSING MY MOST PROFITABLE MODEL.
BUT MOST MODELS ARE PRIMA DONNAS, Y'KNOW? THEY SEE YOU AS NOTHING MORE THAN A MEANS TO AN END, SO YOU TREAT THEM THE SAME WAY. NOT MADISON.
SHE WAS SPECIAL.
THANK YOU FOR YOUR COOPERATION, MR. LARUE. DON'T LEAVE TOWN, PLEASE.
WE'LL BE IN TOUCH.
I MIGHT HAVE BEEN WRONG ABOUT HIM.
THE EVIDENCE MAY TELL US FOR SURE. BUT HE SEEMS SINCERE.
IF IT WASN'T HIM, THOUGH... THEN WHO?

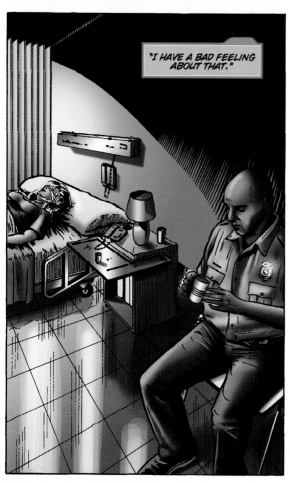

"I HAVE A BAD FEELING ABOUT THAT."

TIME FOR A REFILL. I'LL BE BACK IN A MOMENT, MS. SINGER.

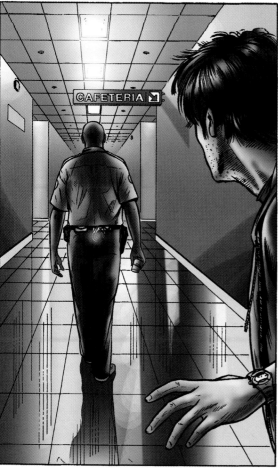

CAFETERIA

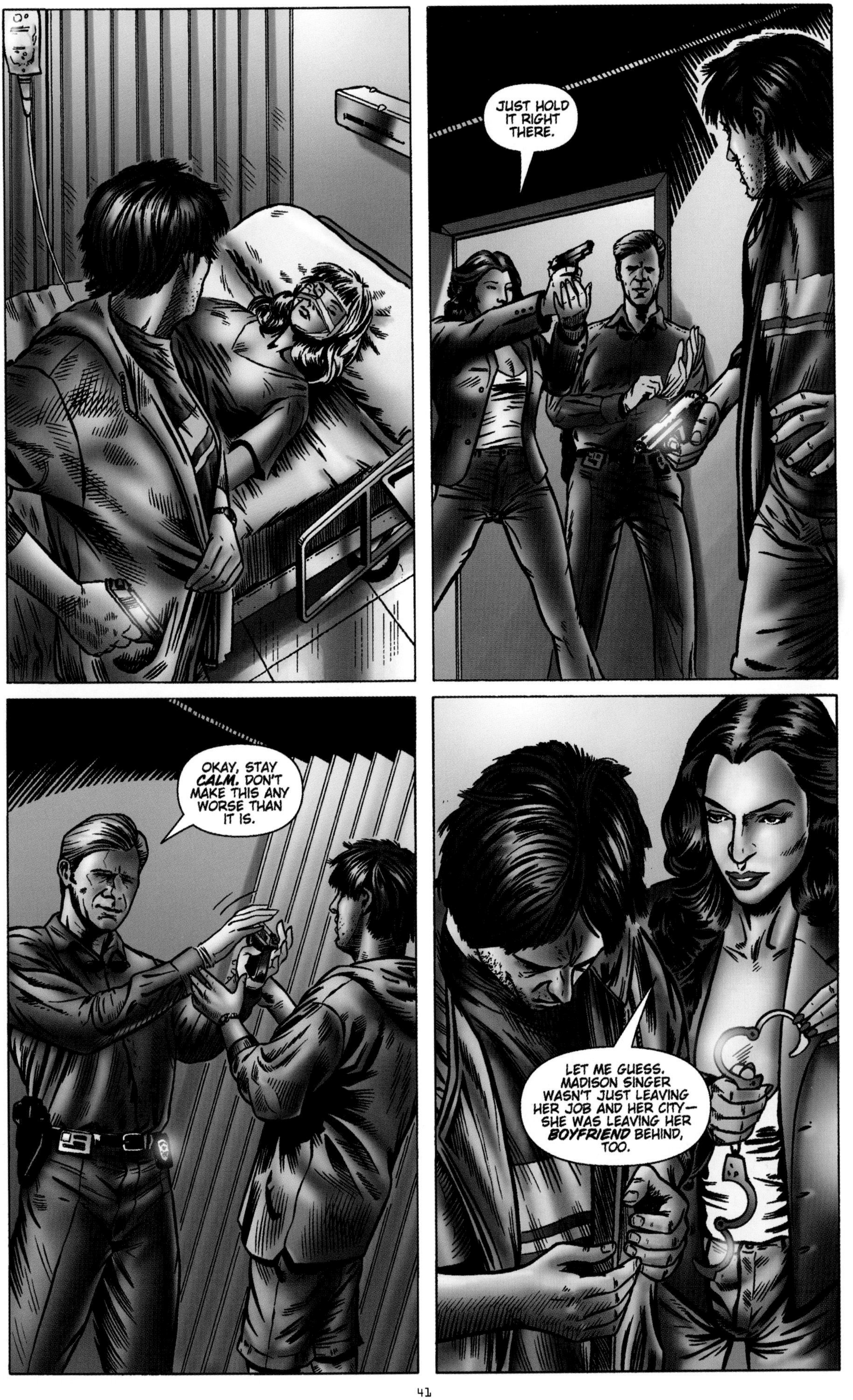
JUST HOLD IT RIGHT THERE.
OKAY, STAY **CALM.** DON'T MAKE THIS ANY WORSE THAN IT IS.
LET ME GUESS. MADISON SINGER WASN'T JUST LEAVING HER JOB AND HER CITY— SHE WAS LEAVING HER ***BOYFRIEND*** BEHIND, TOO.

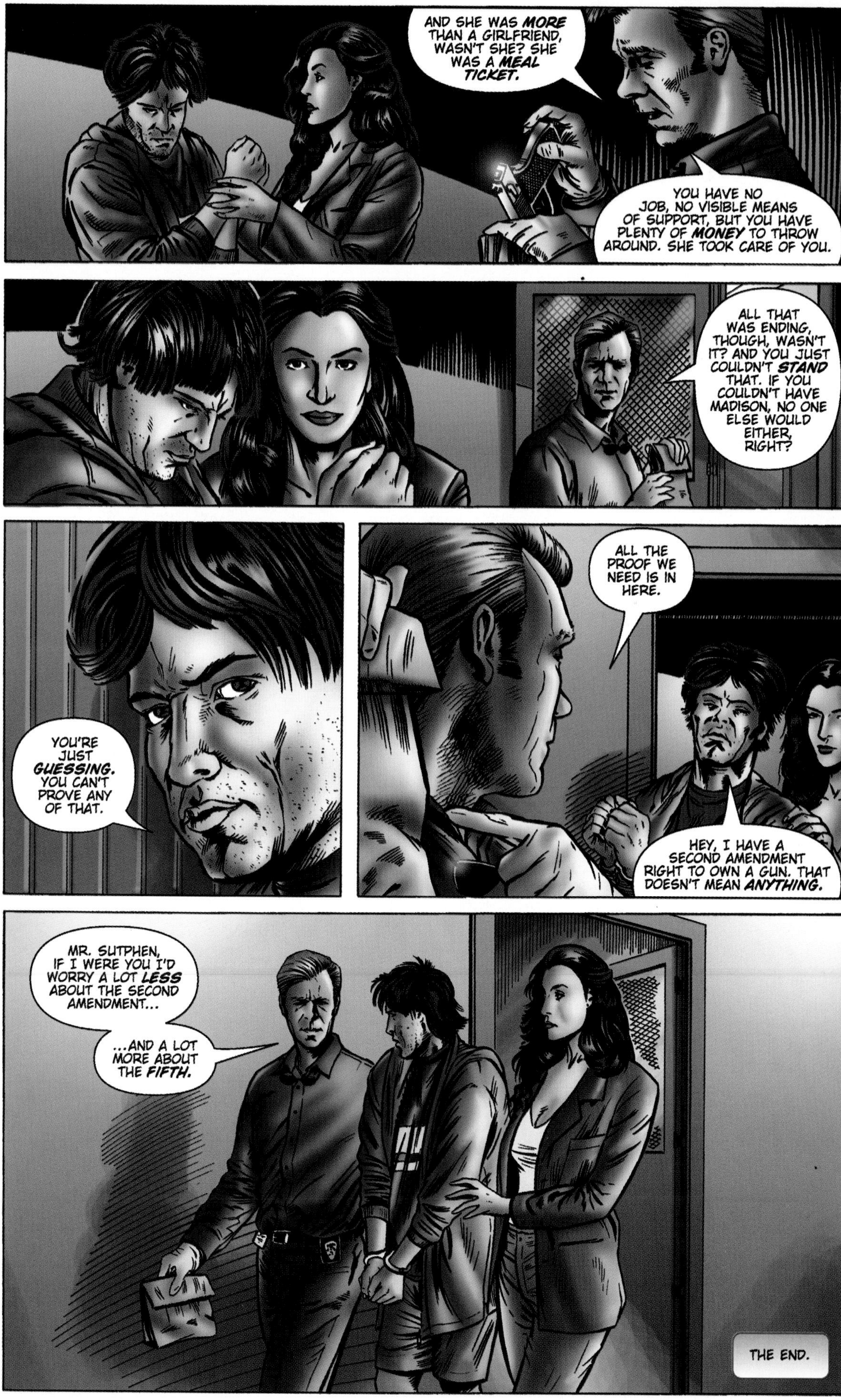

AND SHE WAS MORE THAN A GIRLFRIEND, WASN'T SHE? SHE WAS A MEAL TICKET.
YOU HAVE NO JOB, NO VISIBLE MEANS OF SUPPORT, BUT YOU HAVE PLENTY OF MONEY TO THROW AROUND. SHE TOOK CARE OF YOU.
ALL THAT WAS ENDING, THOUGH, WASN'T IT? AND YOU JUST COULDN'T STAND THAT. IF YOU COULDN'T HAVE MADISON, NO ONE ELSE WOULD EITHER, RIGHT?
YOU'RE JUST GUESSING. YOU CAN'T PROVE ANY OF THAT.
ALL THE PROOF WE NEED IS IN HERE.
HEY, I HAVE A SECOND AMENDMENT RIGHT TO OWN A GUN. THAT DOESN'T MEAN ANYTHING.
MR. SUTPHEN, IF I WERE YOU I'D WORRY A LOT LESS ABOUT THE SECOND AMENDMENT...
...AND A LOT MORE ABOUT THE FIFTH.
THE END.

CSI: Crime Scene Investigation—Bad Rap

In IDW's newest *CSI* comic book miniseries, Grissom and the CSI team are puzzled by the murder of rapper Busta Kapp! The problem isn't that there's no suspect— the problem is that there are too many!

Writer **Max Allan Collins** and artists **Gabriel Rodriguez** and **Ashley Wood** lead readers through the twists and turns of another *CSI* adventure.

A new 5-issue comic book miniseries
On Sale Now

$3.99

www.**idw**publishing.com

Dig deeper...

Read these electrifying original paperback novels based on the Emmy® and Golden Globe® Award-nominated television series!

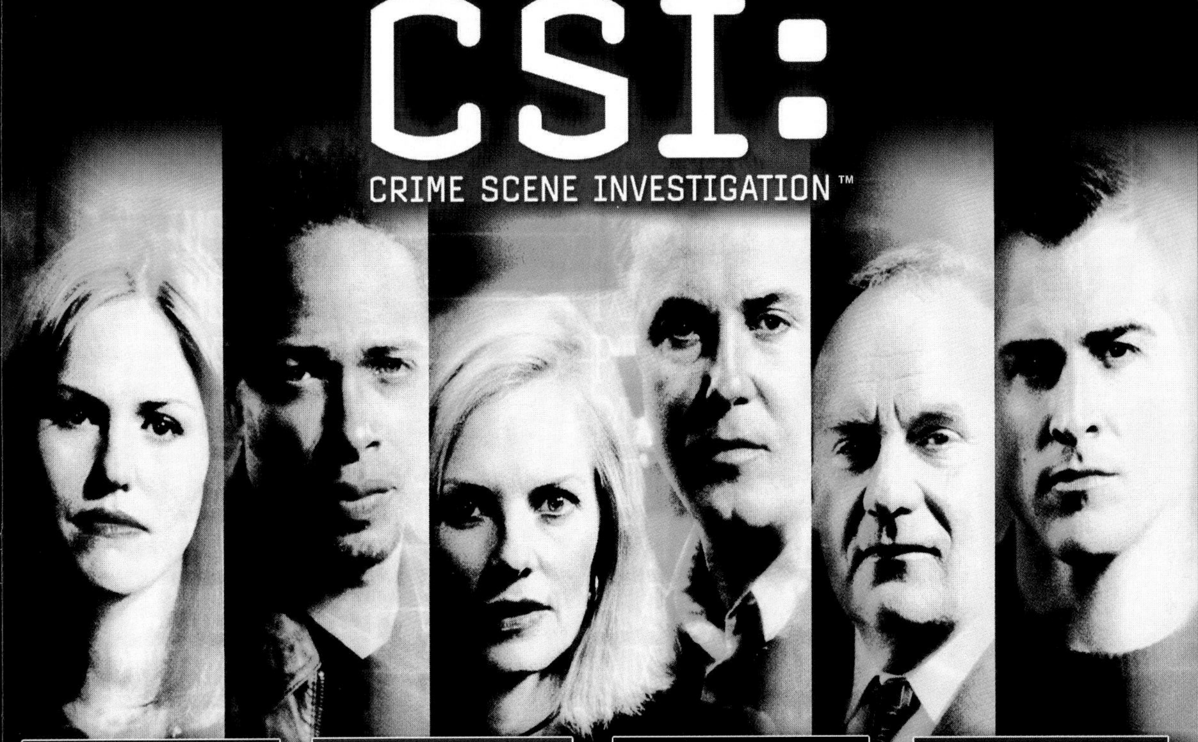

CSI:
CRIME SCENE INVESTIGATION™

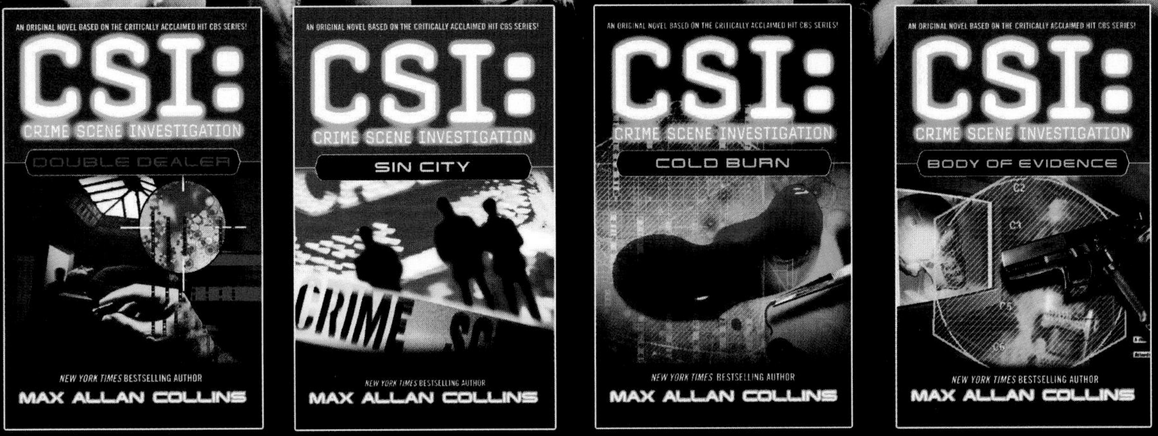

AN ORIGINAL NOVEL BASED ON THE CRITICALLY ACCLAIMED HIT CBS SERIES!
CSI: CRIME SCENE INVESTIGATION
DOUBLE DEALER
NEW YORK TIMES BESTSELLING AUTHOR
MAX ALLAN COLLINS
AN ORIGINAL NOVEL BASED ON THE CRITICALLY ACCLAIMED HIT CBS SERIES!
CSI: CRIME SCENE INVESTIGATION
SIN CITY
NEW YORK TIMES BESTSELLING AUTHOR
MAX ALLAN COLLINS
AN ORIGINAL NOVEL BASED ON THE CRITICALLY ACCLAIMED HIT CBS SERIES!
CSI: CRIME SCENE INVESTIGATION
COLD BURN
NEW YORK TIMES BESTSELLING AUTHOR
MAX ALLAN COLLINS
AN ORIGINAL NOVEL BASED ON THE CRITICALLY ACCLAIMED HIT CBS SERIES!
CSI: CRIME SCENE INVESTIGATION
BODY OF EVIDENCE
NEW YORK TIMES BESTSELLING AUTHOR
MAX ALLAN COLLINS

Riveting and unforgettable thrillers written by

MAX ALLAN COLLINS

Author of the bestselling graphic novel *Road to Perdition*!

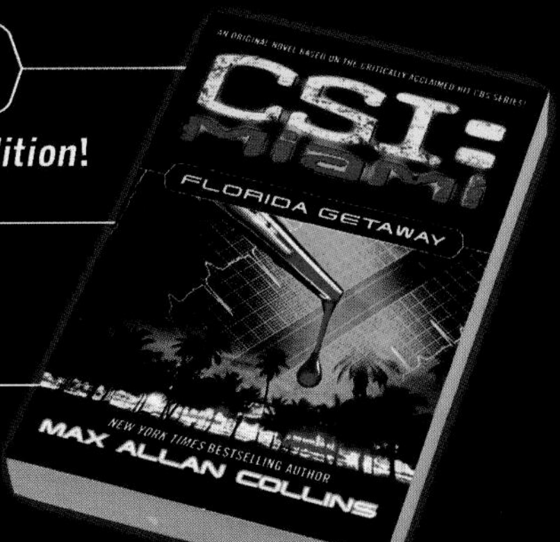

AN ORIGINAL NOVEL BASED ON THE CRITICALLY ACCLAIMED HIT CBS SERIES!
CSI: MIAMI
FLORIDA GETAWAY
NEW YORK TIMES BESTSELLING AUTHOR
MAX ALLAN COLLINS

And look for all new novels based on
CSI: MIAMI™

POCKET STAR BOOKS
A Division of Simon & Schuster
A VIACOM COMPANY
www.simonsays.com

Visit the official website at
www.cbs.com/primetime/csi.

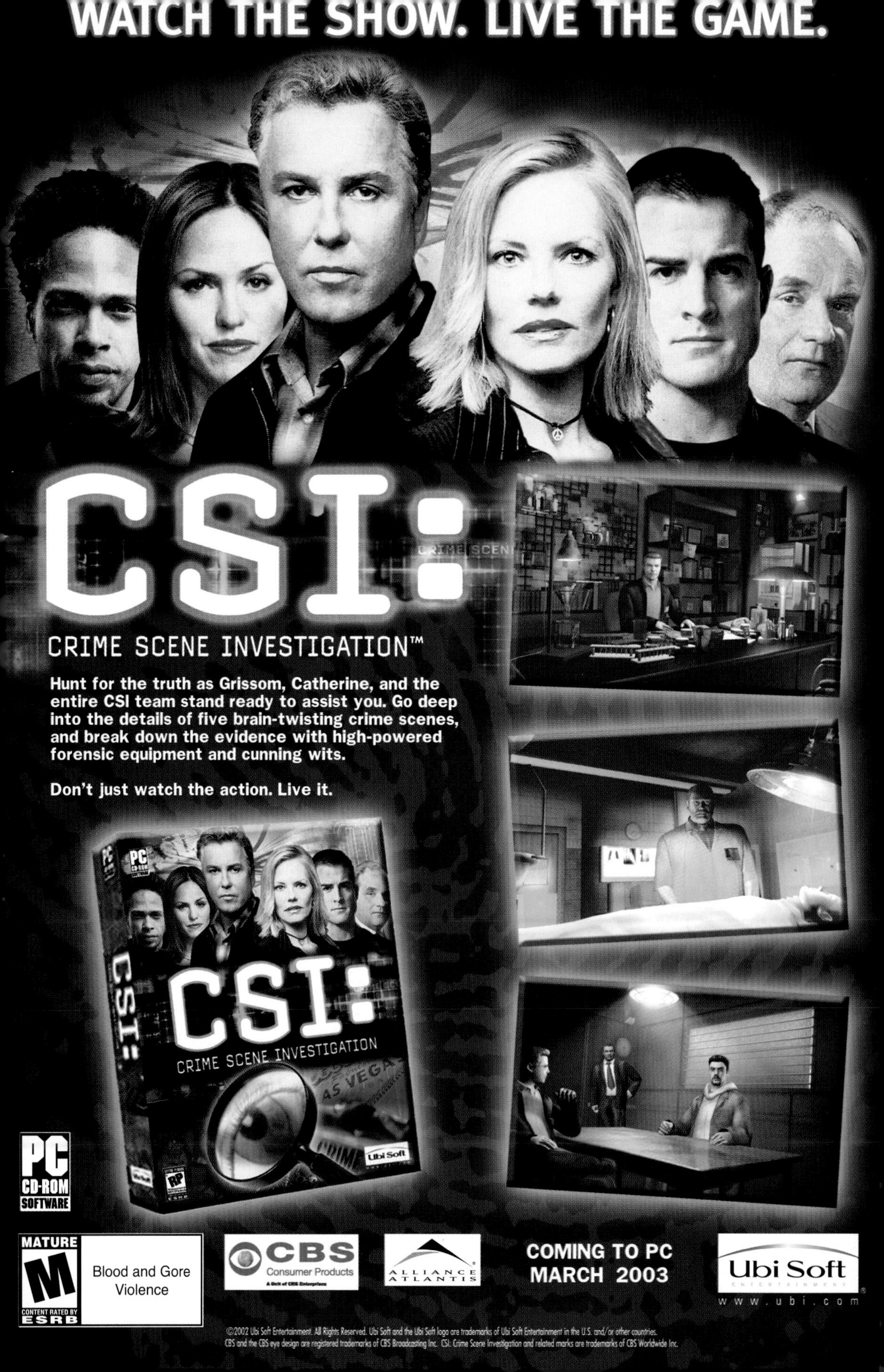

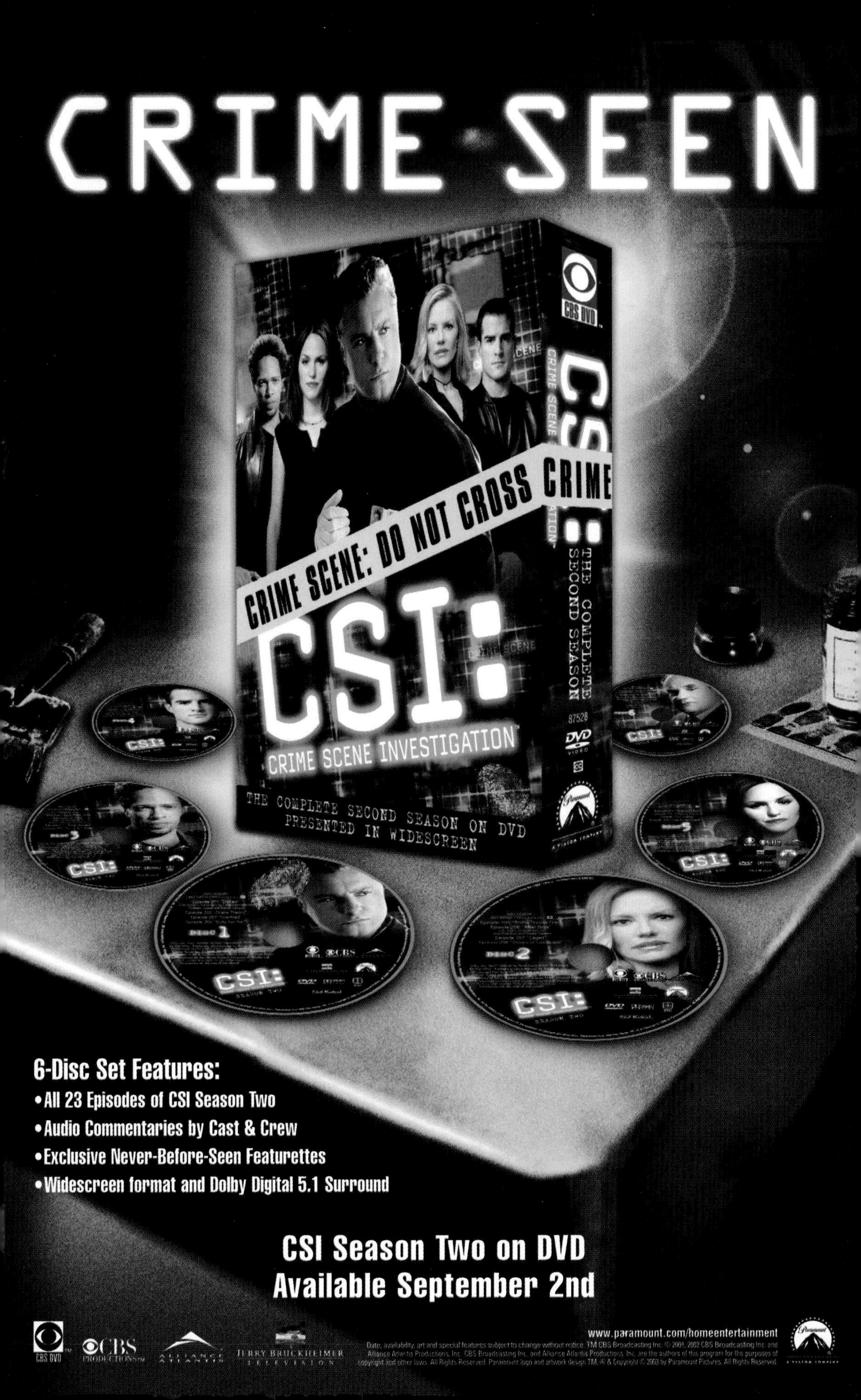
CRIME SEEN
CRIME SCENE: DO NOT CROSS CRIME
CSI:
CRIME SCENE INVESTIGATION
THE COMPLETE SECOND SEASON ON DVD PRESENTED IN WIDESCREEN
CBS DVD
CSI: CRIME SCENE INVESTIGATION
THE COMPLETE SECOND SEASON
6-Disc Set Features:
• All 23 Episodes of CSI Season Two
• Audio Commentaries by Cast & Crew
• Exclusive Never-Before-Seen Featurettes
• Widescreen format and Dolby Digital 5.1 Surround
CSI Season Two on DVD
Available September 2nd
CBS DVD
CBS PRODUCTIONS
ALLIANCE ATLANTIS
JERRY BRUCKHEIMER TELEVISION
www.paramount.com/homeentertainment
Date, availability, art and special features subject to change without notice. TM CBS Broadcasting Inc. © 2001, 2002 CBS Broadcasting Inc. and Alliance Atlantis Productions, Inc. CBS Broadcasting Inc. and Alliance Atlantis Productions, Inc. are the authors of this program for the purposes of copyright and other laws. All Rights Reserved. Paramount logo and artwork design TM, ® & Copyright © 2003 by Paramount Pictures. All Rights Reserved.

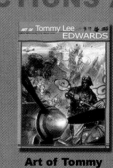

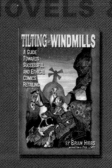